Dreamweaver CS6:
Basic

Student Manual

ACE Edition

D1360866

Dreamweaver CS6: Basic

Chief Executive Officer, Axzo Press:	Ken Wasnock
Series Designer and COO:	Adam A. Wilcox
Vice President, Operations:	Josh Pincus
Director of Publishing Systems Development:	Dan Quackenbush
Writer:	Jim O'Shea
Development assistance:	Linda K. Long
Keytester:	Cliff Coryea

Trademarks

ILT Series is a trademark of Axzo Press.

Some of the product names and company names used in this book have been used for identification purposes only and may be trademarks or registered trademarks of their respective manufacturers and sellers.

Disclaimer

We reserve the right to revise this publication and make changes from time to time in its content without notice.

ISBN 10: 1-4260-3574-8
ISBN 13: 978-1-4260-3574-6

Printed in the United States of America

1 2 3 4 5 GL 06 05 04 03

Contents

Introduction

After reading this introduction, you will know how to:

A Use ILT Series manuals in general.

B Use prerequisites, a target student description, course objectives, and a skills inventory to properly set your expectations for the course.

C Re-key this course after class.

Topic A: About the manual

ILT Series philosophy

Our manuals facilitate your learning by providing structured interaction with the software itself. While we provide text to explain difficult concepts, the hands-on activities are the focus of our courses. By paying close attention as your instructor leads you through these activities, you will learn the skills and concepts effectively.

We believe strongly in the instructor-led class. During class, focus on your instructor. Our manuals are designed and written to facilitate your interaction with your instructor, and not to call attention to manuals themselves.

We believe in the basic approach of setting expectations, delivering instruction, and providing summary and review afterwards. For this reason, lessons begin with objectives and end with summaries. We also provide overall course objectives and a course summary to provide both an introduction to and closure on the entire course.

Manual components

The manuals contain these major components:

- Table of contents
- Introduction
- Units
- Appendix
- Course summary
- Glossary
- Index

Each element is described below.

Table of contents

The table of contents acts as a learning roadmap.

Introduction

The introduction contains information about our training philosophy and our manual components, features, and conventions. It contains target student, prerequisite, objective, and setup information for the specific course.

Units

Units are the largest structural component of the course content. A unit begins with a title page that lists objectives for each major subdivision, or topic, within the unit. Within each topic, conceptual and explanatory information alternates with hands-on activities. Units conclude with a summary comprising one paragraph for each topic, and an independent practice activity that gives you an opportunity to practice the skills you've learned.

The conceptual information takes the form of text paragraphs, exhibits, lists, and tables. The activities are structured in two columns, one telling you what to do, the other providing explanations, descriptions, and graphics.

Appendices

An appendix is similar to a unit in that it contains objectives and conceptual explanations. However, an appendix does not include hands-on activities, a summary, or an independent practice activity.

Course summary

This section provides a text summary of the entire course. It is useful for providing closure at the end of the course. The course summary also indicates the next course in this series, if there is one, and lists additional resources you might find useful as you continue to learn about the software.

Glossary

The glossary provides definitions for all of the key terms used in this course.

Index

The index at the end of this manual makes it easy for you to find information about a particular software component, feature, or concept.

Manual conventions

We've tried to keep the number of elements and the types of formatting to a minimum in the manuals. This aids in clarity and makes the manuals more classically elegant looking. But there are some conventions and icons you should know about.

Item	Description
Italic text	In conceptual text, indicates a new term or feature.
Bold text	In unit summaries, indicates a key term or concept. In an independent practice activity, indicates an explicit item that you select, choose, or type.
`Code font`	Indicates code or syntax.
`Longer strings of ▶ code will look ▶ like this.`	In the hands-on activities, any code that's too long to fit on a single line is divided into segments by one or more continuation characters (▶). This code should be entered as a continuous string of text.
Select **bold item**	In the left column of hands-on activities, bold sans-serif text indicates an explicit item that you select, choose, or type.
Keycaps like ↵ ENTER	Indicate a key on the keyboard you must press.

Hands-on activities

The hands-on activities are the most important parts of our manuals. They are divided into two primary columns. The "Here's how" column gives short instructions to you about what to do. The "Here's why" column provides explanations, graphics, and clarifications. Here's a sample:

Do it!

A-1:   Creating a commission formula

Here's how	Here's why
1 Open Sales	This is an oversimplified sales compensation worksheet. It shows sales totals, commissions, and incentives for five sales reps.
2 Observe the contents of cell F4	F4 ▼ = =E4*C_Rate The commission rate formulas use the name "C_Rate" instead of a value for the commission rate.

For these activities, we have provided a collection of data files designed to help you learn each skill in a real-world business context. As you work through the activities, you will modify and update these files. Of course, you might make a mistake and therefore want to re-key the activity starting from scratch. To make it easy to start over, you will rename each data file at the end of the first activity in which the file is modified. Our convention for renaming files is to add the word "My" to the beginning of the file name. In the above activity, for example, a file called "Sales" is being used for the first time. At the end of this activity, you would save the file as "My sales," thus leaving the "Sales" file unchanged. If you make a mistake, you can start over using the original "Sales" file.

In some activities, however, it might not be practical to rename the data file. If you want to retry one of these activities, ask your instructor for a fresh copy of the original data file.

Topic B: Setting your expectations

Properly setting your expectations is essential to your success. This topic will help you do that by providing:

- Prerequisites for this course
- A description of the target student
- A list of the objectives for the course
- A skills assessment for the course

Course prerequisites

Before taking this course, you should be familiar with personal computers and the use of a keyboard and a mouse. Furthermore, this course assumes that you've completed the following courses or have equivalent experience:

- *Windows 7: Basic, Windows Vista: Basic, or Windows XP: Basic*

Target student

This course will benefit students who want to learn how to use Dreamweaver CS6 to create and modify websites. You will learn how to plan, define, and create a website; add pages and content; format text; create and apply CSS styles; create links; manage images and other files; and publish a site. You should take this course if you are comfortable using a PC and have experience with Microsoft Windows 7, Vista, or XP. You should have little or no experience with Dreamweaver.

Adobe ACE certification

This course is designed to help you pass the Adobe Certified Expert (ACE) exam for Dreamweaver CS6. For complete certification training, you should complete this course and *Dreamweaver CS6: Advanced, ACE Edition.*

Course objectives

These overall course objectives will give you an idea about what to expect from the course. It is also possible that they will help you see that this course is not the right one for you. If you think you either lack the prerequisite knowledge or already know most of the subject matter to be covered, you should let your instructor know that you think you are misplaced in the class.

After completing this course, you will know how to:

- Understand basic Internet and HTML concepts; identify the components of the Dreamweaver CS6 workspace; create a custom workspace; use the Property inspector; and preview pages in a browser.

- Plan and define a Web site; create new web pages; and work with the Files panel to organize site files.

- Insert and import text to a web page; insert special characters; define a basic page structure; insert line breaks, and create lists.

- Use CSS to format a website; create external style sheets; create and apply class styles, and use the cascade effect to their advantage.

- Add image placeholders, images, and rollover images to a web page; perform basic image editing in Dreamweaver; add Flash files; and connect web pages with links..

- Understand basic HTML code concepts; add content to the <head> section; use the Code Navigator, tag selector, and options on the Coding toolbar; use the Quick Tag Editor; and replace text and code by using the Find and Replace dialog box.

- Check file size and download times; check for spelling errors; check for broken links and orphaned files; cloak files; connect to a remote server; upload and update a site; and use the Check In and Check Out feature.

Skills inventory

Use the following form to gauge your skill level entering the class. For each skill listed, rate your familiarity from 1 to 5, with five being the most familiar. *This is not a test.* Rather, it is intended to provide you with an idea of where you're starting from at the beginning of class. If you're wholly unfamiliar with all the skills, you might not be ready for the class. If you think you already understand all of the skills, you might need to move on to the next course in the series. In either case, you should let your instructor know as soon as possible.

Skill	1	2	3	4	5
Understanding basic HTML, XHTML, and HTML5 concepts					
Identifying components of the Dreamweaver CS6 workspace					
Creating a custom workspace					
Using the Workspace Switcher					
Inserting, editing, and formatting text					
Switching between document views					
Setting the page title					
Previewing pages in a browser					
Applying planning tools such as flowcharts and wireframes					
Understanding basic design principles					
Defining a local site					
Creating new web pages					
Working with the Files panel					
Inserting and importing text from external files					
Inserting special characters					
Defining a page structure					
Inserting line breaks					
Creating unordered, ordered, and definition lists					
Understanding CSS basics					
Creating and attaching external style sheets					
Creating and applying class styles					

Skill	1	2	3	4	5
Understanding the cascade effect					
Inserting images, placeholders, and rollovers					
Editing images in Dreamweaver and in an external image editor					
Adding Flash files					
Understanding how links work					
Creating links to other pages and resources					
Creating named anchors and linking to them					
Creating e-mail links					
Applying CSS styles to link states					
Defining keywords and description in the `<head>` section					
Using the Code Navigator and tag selector to select code element					
Using options on the Coding toolbar to add and modify code					
Using the Quick Tag Editor to add and edit HTML tags					
Using the Find and Replace dialog box to update content and code					
Checking file size and download times					
Checking for spelling errors					
Fixing broken links					
Locating orphaned files					
Cloaking files and folders					
Connecting to a remote server					
Uploading and updating a site					
Checking in and checking out files					

Topic C: **Re-keying the course**

If you have the proper hardware and software, you can re-key this course after class. This section explains what you'll need in order to do so, and how to do it.

Hardware requirements

Your personal computer should have:

- A keyboard and a mouse
- An Intel Pentium 4, Intel Centrino, Intel Xeon, or Intel Core Duo (or compatible) processor
- At least 1 GB of RAM
- 1 GB of hard disk space for Dreamweaver CS6 installation; additional space needed for operating system and Office installation
- A DVD-ROM drive for installation
- A monitor set to a minimum resolution of 1280 × 960 and 24-bit color or better

Software requirements

You will also need the following software:

- Windows 7 (You can also use Windows Vista, or Windows XP with Service Pack 3, but the screen shots in this course were taken using Windows 7, so your screens might look somewhat different.)
- Adobe Dreamweaver CS6.

  Note: This course was designed using the Adobe Creative Cloud subscription version of Dreamweaver CS6 (version 12.2 build 6006). If you key this course in a different version or build, your screens might look somewhat different and activities might not key as written.
- Adobe Fireworks CS6 (required to complete optional activity B-2 in the "Images, multimedia, and links" unit)
- Microsoft Outlook, Thunderbird, or another e-mail client (required to complete Activity E-3 in the "Images, multimedia, and links" unit)
- Microsoft Word 2000 or later version (required to complete Activity A-1 in the "Basic editing" unit)
- Updated versions of the Internet Explorer and Firefox browsers.

Network requirements

The following network components and connectivity are also required for re-keying this course:

- Internet access, for the following purposes:
  - Downloading the latest critical updates and service packs
  - Visiting and discussing designs on the Web, and completing Activity E-3 in the "Images, multimedia, and links" unit
  - Downloading the Student Data files (if necessary)

Setup instructions to re-key the course

Before you re-key the course, you will need to perform the following steps.

1 Use Windows Update to install all available critical updates and Service Packs.

2 With flat-panel displays, we recommend using the panel's native resolution for best results. Color depth/quality should be set to High (24 bit) or higher.

Please note that your display settings or resolution may differ from the author's, so your screens might not exactly match the screen shots in this manual.

3 If necessary, reset any Dreamweaver CS6 defaults that you have changed. If you do not wish to reset the defaults, you can still re-key the course, but some activities might not work exactly as documented.

4 If you have the data disc that came with this manual, locate the Student Data folder on it and copy it to the desktop of your computer.

If you don't have the data disc, you can download the Student Data files for the course:

   a Connect to http://downloads.logicaloperations.com.
   b Enter the course title or search by part to locate this course
   c Click the course title to display a list of available downloads.
      Note: Data Files are located under the Instructor Edition of the course.
   d Click the link(s) for downloading the Student Data files.
   e Create a folder named Student Data on the desktop of your computer.
   f Double-click the downloaded zip file(s) and drag the contents into the Student Data folder.

U n i t   1

Getting started

Complete this unit, and you'll know how to:

A Discuss basic Internet, HTML, and XHTML concepts.

B Identify components of the Dreamweaver CS6 workspace, and create a custom workspace.

C Switch views, specify page titles, and make basic edits using features and tools in the Document window.

D Use the Property inspector to set element properties.

E Preview a web page in a browser and set the primary and secondary preview browsers.

Topic A: The Internet and website planning

Explanation

Before you start using Dreamweaver CS6 to design and create websites, you should first understand the basics of the Internet, the Web, and HTML.

The Internet and the Web

The *Internet* is a vast array of networks that belong to universities, businesses, organizations, governments, and individuals all over the world. The World Wide Web, or simply the *Web*, is one of many services of the Internet. Some other Internet services include e-mail, File Transfer Protocol (FTP), and instant messaging.

To view web pages and other content, you need a *web browser*, such as Google Chrome, Firefox, Internet Explorer, or Safari. Web content typically includes text, images, and multimedia files. Each page or resource has a unique address known as a *Uniform Resource Locater* (URL).

A *website* is a collection of linked pages. The top-level page is commonly called the *Home page*. A home page typically provides hyperlinks to navigate to other pages within the site or to external pages. A *hyperlink*—or more commonly, a *link*—is text or an image that, when clicked, takes the user to another page, another location on the current page, another website, or a specific file.

HTML

Hypertext Markup Language, or *HTML*, is the standard markup language used on the Web to create web pages. HTML enables you to structure your website's content. An HTML document is a plain text file that contains HTML code, along with the content for a web page. Exhibit 1-1 shows the code for a simple HTML document and how that document displays in a web browser. HTML documents have an .htm or .html file extension.

HTML uses elements to define the basic structure of a web page. These elements enclose the content using tag syntax. A web page can contain links, images, multimedia files, and other elements. When a browser opens a web page, the text typically loads quickly, while images and embedded media files might take longer.

The current standard for HTML is HTML 4.01, which was published in December 1999. Currently, there is intensive work being done to define its next version, HTML5. Some web browsers already support some of the new elements provided in HTML5.

XHTML

Extensible Hypertext Markup Language, or *XHTML*, is a more efficient and strict version of HTML. For years, browser makers introduced proprietary tags and attributes in an effort to give web designers more control over the look and feel of their web pages. Unfortunately, most of these elements and attributes served only to make web page code bloated, cluttered, and semantically meaningless. Because XHTML doesn't allow proprietary tags or attributes, the result is cleaner, more efficient code that is more evenly supported across different browsers. Dreamweaver CS6 builds web pages with XHTML code by default.

```
<!DOCTYPE html PUBLIC "-//W3C//DTD XHTML 1.0 Transitional//EN"
"http://www.w3.org/TR/xhtml1/DTD/xhtml1-transitional.dtd">
<html xmlns="http://www.w3.org/1999/xhtml">
<head>
<meta http-equiv="Content-Type" content="text/html; charset=utf-8" />
<title>Harvest Valley Market</title>
</head>

<body>
<p><img src="images/harvest-valley-market-logo1.jpg" width="200" height="125"
 alt="Harvest Valley Market Logo" />
</p>
<p>Welcome to Harvest Valley Market!</p>
</body>
</html>
```

Exhibit 1-1: A simple web page shown as XHTML code and in a browser

Do it!   **A-1:   Discussing the Web, HTML, and XHTML**

Questions and answers
1   What's the difference between the Internet and the World Wide Web?
2   What other Internet services are there?
3   What's a web page?
4   What's a website?
5   What's a web browser?
6   What's HTML?
7   What's XHTML?
8   What version of HTML is being developed?

Website planning

Explanation

When you start a new website, it's important to first plan the site project carefully before you begin developing the design and content.

Basic elements of a site plan

When you plan your website's design, consider more than your visual design approach. Other factors, including accessibility, structure, navigation, and consistent rendering in multiple browsers, are equally important.

Also, a critical component of any web development project is an analysis of the site's purpose and its intended audience. More specifically, keep these factors in mind before you begin development:

- **Audience** — Analyze the interests, age, experiences, background, and expectations of your audience. You'll find that many of your later design choices are based on this analysis.

- **Purpose** — Determine the purpose for your website. The purpose is determined by the goals you want to accomplish with the site.

- **Content** — Assemble content that clearly conveys the purpose of the site and makes sure it is relevant to the intended users. The language, tone, graphics, and level of detail should be based on an analysis of the site's objectives and target audience.

- **Site structure** — Finalize the navigation structure at the beginning of the design process. Changing the site structure later can be costly and time consuming.

Analyzing a site's audience and purpose

It's important to spend some time defining the audience for the site and the goals you want to accomplish with the site. Ask yourself or your team the following general questions as part of a comprehensive (and ongoing) analysis:

- Who are we trying to reach, and what are the audience demographics—the education level, age range, gender, or special interests of the target audience?

- What does the intended audience already know about the information that will be presented on the site?

- What values or experiences might members of this audience have in common?

- What do we (or the client) want to achieve with the site?

- What are the client's goals?

- How will the site achieve the established goals?

- What information will the audience be looking for on the website?

- How will we keep visitors interested and engaged over the long term?

- What are the specific needs of the site's users, and how will we tailor the design and content to those needs?

- Which browsers are predominantly used by the target audience?

- What Internet access speed is typical, on average, for the target audience?

Design considerations

You can attract and retain users by designing pages that make it easy for them to find the information they're looking for. You can do this with a blend of colors, graphics, content, and navigational aids. Before you begin actual design and content work, think about how best to structure the site's content and how you want to present information.

When you plan a site's design and structure, keep the following factors in mind:

- **Navigation** — Create a navigation scheme that makes it easy for the audience to decipher the site's structure, and it should be consistent on every page.

- **Fonts** — Choose fonts that provide optimal readability and that suit the target audience. For example, you might use standard fonts, such as Verdana and Georgia for a corporate site, but a more playful font, such as Comic Sans MS, for a site targeted to kids.

- **Page length** — Break information into manageable chunks. A page that contains excessive text and requires a lot of vertical scrolling can be tedious to users.

- **Visual contrast** — Make sure your background color and text color have sufficient contrast so that the text is clear, crisp, and easy to read.

- **Load time** — Use graphics and other potentially "heavy" components conservatively. You can lose visitors if it takes too long for your pages to load.

- **Headings** — Use headings carefully. They should serve as titles or brief descriptors for the content beneath them.

Do it!   **A-2:   Discussing basic design considerations**

Questions and answers

1 What are some important factors to consider when planning a website?

2 What content factors are important to consider when planning a site?

3 What questions can you ask yourself or your project team to help ensure that content and design choices stay relevant to the site's overall purpose?

4 You have determined that your site's audience is composed solely of people in a corporation using high-speed access and a standard browser. What design decisions might be affected by this information?

5 Why is it important to choose background colors and text colors carefully?

6 Why is it important to break text into logical, manageable chunks?

Topic B: Setting up your workspace

This topic covers the following Adobe ACE exam objectives for Dreamweaver CS6.

#	Objective
1.4	Configure workspace layout
1.4.1	Applying the pre-configured workspace layouts
1.4.2	Customizing personalized workspace layouts

Developing websites in Dreamweaver CS6

Explanation

Dreamweaver CS6 is web authoring software that helps you design and create websites and applications. When you create or change a page in the Dreamweaver workspace, Dreamweaver automatically generates the required XHTML, CSS, or scripting code. You can also write or edit code manually. Before you get started creating websites, you should become familiar with the Dreamweaver CS6 interface.

Starting Dreamweaver and opening a file

When you start Dreamweaver, the Welcome screen appears, as shown in Exhibit 1-2. This screen provides a starting point where you can open recently opened files, create a new web page, view instructional videos, and access online help. Under Create New, you can click any option to open a new blank file of the selected type. For example, click HTML to open a new, blank HTML page. You can start building from this blank page, or you can close it and open an existing file. If you don't want the Welcome screen to appear the next time you start Dreamweaver, check Don't show again (at the bottom of the screen), and click OK.

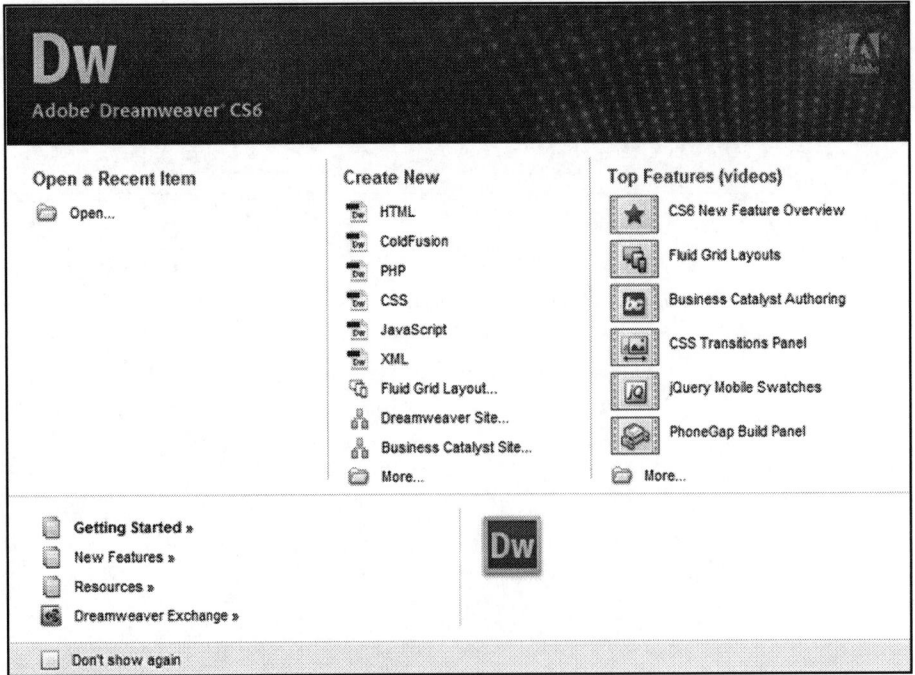

Exhibit 1-2: The Dreamweaver CS6 Welcome screen

To open an existing file, choose File, Open and browse to locate the file you want to open. Select the file and click Open, or double-click the file.

To start a new file, choose File, New. The New Document dialog box opens, with the blank HTML page option selected by default. Click Create to start a new HTML page.

Workspace components

The default Dreamweaver CS6 workspace is shown in Exhibit 1-3. A workspace is a window that contains various components with different functions. The composition of the workspace can be customized depending on the needs of the user. The default workspace includes the Application bar at the top of the window, the Document toolbar, the Document window (where you perform most of your work), the panel groups (which include the Files panel shown in the bottom-right corner), and the Property inspector (also called the Properties panel).

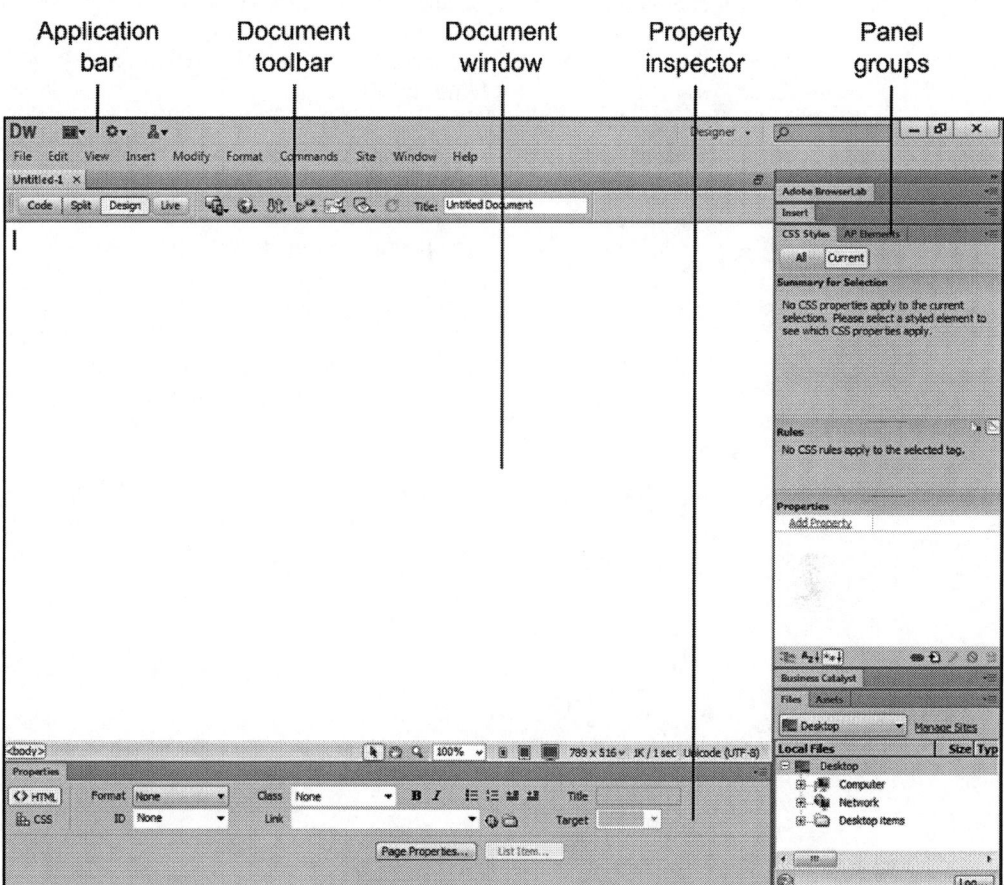

Exhibit 1-3: The default Dreamweaver CS6 workspace

The following table describes the main components of the Dreamweaver CS6 workspace.

Component	Description
Application bar	Contains application controls, the Workspace Switcher, and menus.
Document toolbar	Provides buttons you can use to perform a variety of common tasks. For example, you can switch between views, check for errors, and enable and disable various visual aids.
Document window	Displays the current page. This is where you'll do most of your work. You can switch among Design, Code, Split, Live, and Live Code views.
Panel groups	Contain a set of panels. Panels contain collections of related options and commands to help you monitor and edit your files. For example, two frequently used panels are the Insert panel and the Files panel.
Insert panel (or Insert bar)	Provides buttons you can use to quickly insert elements, such as images, links, tables, and Div tags, into a document. You can convert the Insert panel into a horizontal bar for quick access to frequently used elements.
Files panel	Displays your site folders and files. You can open a file by double-clicking it in the Files panel, or move files by dragging them between folders. You can also drag a file from the Files panel to the Document window to open it, and you can rename, delete, and copy files from within the Files panel.
Property inspector	(Also called the Properties panel.) Displays the properties of the selected element. The options and commands that appear change based on what's selected in the Document window.

Do it!

B-1:   Identifying workspace components

The files for this activity are in Student Data folder **Unit 1\Topic B**.

Here's how	Here's why
1 Click **Start** and choose **All Programs**, **Adobe Dreamweaver CS6**	To start Dreamweaver CS6. If the Default Editor dialog box appears, click OK.
2 At the bottom of the Welcome screen, check **Don't show again**	To prevent the welcome screen from appearing the next time Dreamweaver CS6 starts. A dialog box appears, indicating that you can enable the Welcome screen again later if necessary.
Click **OK**	The Welcome screen remains open.
3 Choose **File, Open...**	
Browse to the current topic folder	It is in the current unit folder in the Student Data folder.
Open the **Harvest Valley Market** folder	
Double-click **index.html**	To open the Harvest Valley Market Home page in the Document window.
Observe the Document window title bar	(At the top of the Document window.) The path to the open file is shown for reference.
4 Locate the Application bar and observe the Workspace Switcher	The default workspace is Designer.
On the Application bar, click as shown	
	To display workspace layout views and options for the Document window.

5 On the menu bar, click **File**	To open the File menu. The drop-down menus in the menu bar contain commands for performing a wide variety of tasks.
With the menu open, point to **Edit**	(The next item in the menu bar.) To display the commands in the Edit menu.
Point to **View**	To display the commands in the View menu.
Briefly explore the other menus	
6 Locate the Document toolbar	The Document toolbar contains buttons that control the current view of the open web page. The toolbar also displays the page title and provides buttons and pop-up menus for frequently used commands.
7 At the top of the Panel groups, click **Insert**, as shown	
	To expand the Insert panel. Using the Insert panel, you can quickly add elements to a page. The buttons in this panel are shortcuts to the commands in the Insert menu.
Double-click **Insert**	To collapse the panel.
8 Locate the Property inspector	The Property inspector displays attributes and options for the selected page element. You can quickly edit properties such as text alignment and font styles.
9 Locate the Files panel	The Files panel is collapsed by default in the Designer workspace.

Workspace layouts

Explanation

Dreamweaver CS6 provides eleven preset workspace layouts designed to suit different types of developers or projects. The layouts are App Developer, App Developer Plus, Business Catalyst, Classic, Coder, Coder Plus, Designer (the default workspace), Designer Compact, Dual Screen, Fluid Layout, and Mobile Applications. Each layout is optimized for its purpose. For example, the Coder workspace is for developers who need to edit code and use code snippets and other assets. You can also create a custom workspace to suit your development preferences.

The Workspace Switcher

To switch workspace layouts, click the Workspace Switcher button in the Application bar and choose a layout from the menu, as shown in Exhibit 1-4.

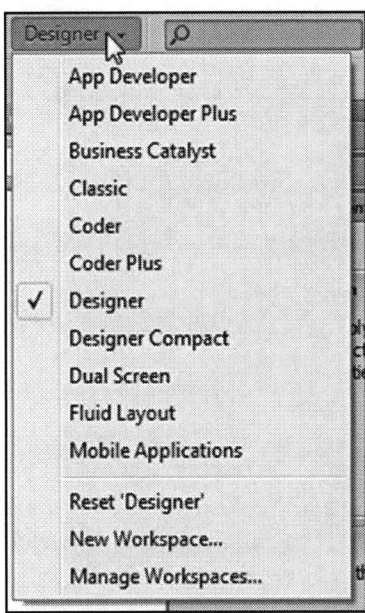

Exhibit 1-4: The Workspace Switcher

You can reset a modified workspace to its original layout by choosing Reset *'Workspace Name'* (for instance, Reset 'Coder') from the Workspace Switcher menu.

Do it!

B-2:   Selecting a workspace layout

The files for this activity are in Student Data folder **Unit 1\Topic B**.

Here's how	Here's why
1 From the Workspace Switcher, select **Classic**	To switch to the Classic workspace layout. This layout has the Insert panel converted to a horizontal bar and the Files panel is now expanded.
2 From the Workspace Switcher, select **Coder**	To switch to the Coder workspace. This layout has Code view as the default view and the panels are positioned on the left side of the Document window.
On the Document toolbar, click **Design**	To switch to Design view.
From the Workspace Switcher, select **Reset 'Coder'**	To reset the Coder workspace back to its original layout.
3 Explore the other workspaces	
4 Switch to the **Designer** workspace	

Panels and panel groups

Explanation

Each workspace layout has its own set and arrangement of panels. For example, the Designer workspace layout displays two panel groups by default: Files and CSS Styles.

Panel tab

Exhibit 1-5: The Files panel group, with the Files panel tab active

You can show, hide, and rearrange panels to customize your workspace. To hide or display a panel, choose Window and then choose a panel. A check mark in the Window menu indicates when a panel is open.

Expanding and collapsing panels

To expand a panel, click its tab. To expand a panel group, click any tab within its group. To collapse a panel, double-click its tab. To collapse a panel group, double-click any tab within the group.

Floating and docking panels

To undock, or "float," a panel group, drag it by its title bar to a desired location. To resize a floating panel, you can point to one of its edges until the pointer changes to a double-sided arrow and then drag to resize the panel.

A floating panel can be docked to the right, left, or bottom of the workspace. To dock a floating panel, drag it by its title bar to the edge where you want to dock. When the blue drop zone appears, release the mouse button.

Grouping, reordering, and stacking panels

You can create custom groups by dragging one panel tab into another. When you've moved the panel to the correct position, a blue drop zone appears. Release the mouse button to add the panel to the new group. To reorder the tabs in a group, drag the tab to the desired position.

To stack panels, drag a panel by its title bar above or below another panel. When the blue line appears, release the mouse button. To minimize a stacked panel down to icons, double-click the stack's title bar or click the double arrows in the

Converting the Insert panel to a horizontal Insert bar

You can convert the Insert panel to a horizontal bar for quick access to frequently used elements and commands. To do so, drag the Insert panel tab above the Document window. A blue line appears, indicating where the Insert bar will be placed. Release the mouse button to place the Insert bar.

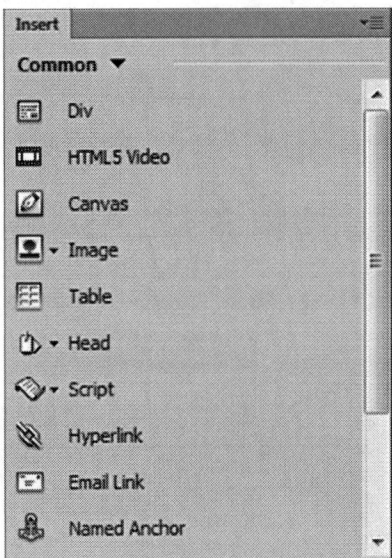

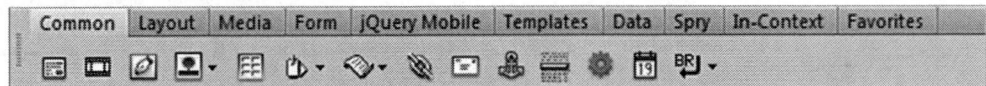

Exhibit 1-6: The Insert panel and the Insert bar

By default, the Insert bar appears as a row of tabs that provide access to related commands. To switch the Insert bar from a tab-based layout to a single bar with a menu for switching categories, right-click the Insert bar and choose Show as Menu. The default category is Common; it includes frequently used elements such as links, tables, and images. To switch back to a tabbed layout, click Common (or the currently selected category) and choose Show as Tabs.

To convert the Insert bar back to a panel, drag from its gripper (the row of small dots) and drop it where your panels are docked.

Do it!

B-3: Managing panels and panel groups

The files for this activity are in Student Data folder **Unit 1\Topic B**.

Here's how	Here's why
1 Choose **Window**, **Assets**	To activate the Assets panel.
Choose **Window**, **Tag Inspector**	(Or press F9.) To activate the Tag Inspector panel.
2 Right-click **Tag Inspector**	(In the Panel groups.) To display a shortcut menu.
Choose **Close**	To close the panel.
3 To the right of the Insert panel, click as shown	
	To display a menu.
Choose **Close**	

4 Choose **Window**, **Insert**	(Or press Ctrl+F2.) To display the expanded panel. Next, you'll move the Insert tab.
5 Drag the **Insert** tab to the Document window	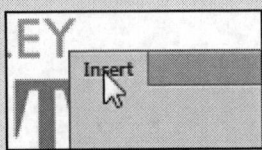
	Click, hold the mouse button, and drag away from the Panel group as shown. Don't release the mouse button.
Point as shown	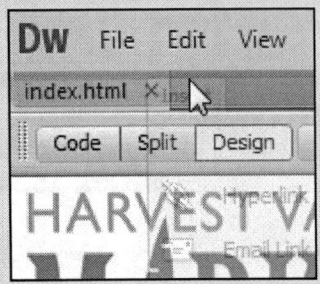
	To display the blue drop area under the Menu bar and above the Document toolbar.
Release the mouse button	To convert the Insert panel into the Insert bar.
6 Right-click the **Insert bar**, as shown	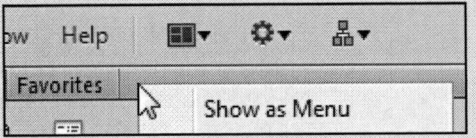
	To display a shortcut menu.
Choose **Show as Menu**	To switch the Insert bar from a tab-based layout to a single bar with a menu. The Common category is displayed by default.
7 Click **Common**, as shown	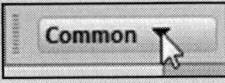
Choose **Layout**	To switch to the Layout category.
8 Click **Layout**	On the Insert bar.
Choose **Show as Tabs**	To switch the Insert bar from a menu into a tab-based layout.
Click **Common**	To switch to the Common category.

9 Point as shown

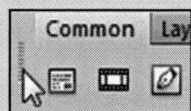

These dotted lines are called the "gripper." You can drag from the gripper to move items in the workspace.

Drag the Insert tab above the CSS Styles panel

Release the mouse when the blue drop area appears

To convert the Insert bar into the Insert panel.

10 Point as shown

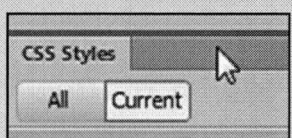

The blank area to the right of the AP Elements tab.

Drag to the Document window, as shown

To the Document window.

Release the mouse

To make it a floating panel.

11 Drag the CSS Styles tab to the Files/Assets panel group, as shown

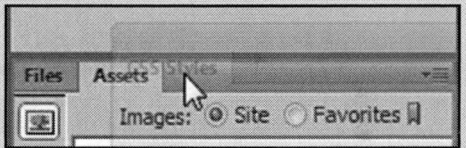

To move the tab to a different panel group.

Drag the CSS Styles tab back to the document window

To make it a floating panel.

12 Click as shown

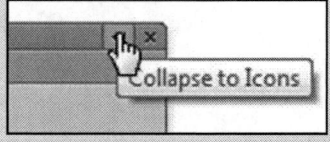

To collapse the CSS Styles panel to icons.

Drag the collapsed CSS Styles panel by its title bar back to the Panel Group

Place it above the Files/Assets panel and below the Insert panel. A blue line shows precisely where the panel group will be placed.

13 Verify the **CSS Styles** panel is expanded

Click its tab, if necessary.

Custom workspaces

Explanation

In addition to using the default workspace layouts, you can arrange any workspace layout to suit your specific needs and save that layout for repeated use. To create a custom workspace layout:

1 Arrange the panels and toolbars in the workspace as desired.

2 From the Workspace Switcher menu, choose New Workspace to open the New Workspace dialog box.

3 Enter a descriptive name for the workspace and click OK. The new workspace name appears at the top of the Workspace Switcher menu.

You can rename or delete custom workspaces by choosing Manage Workspaces from the Workspace Switcher menu. This opens the Manage Workspaces dialog box, which contains a list of custom workspaces (if any).

Do it!

B-4: Creating a custom workspace

The files for this activity are in Student Data folder **Unit 1\Topic B**.

Here's how	Here's why
1 Point to the right edge of the Document window, as shown	
	The pointer changes to a double-sided arrow, indicating that you can resize the window.
Drag to the right	To enlarge the Document window and narrow the panels slightly.
2 Move the Insert panel to the area under the Menu bar and above the Document toolbar	The Insert panel becomes the Insert bar.
3 From the Workspace Switcher menu, choose **New Workspace...**	To open the New Workspace dialog box.
Type **My workspace**	
Click **OK**	The workspace name appears as the active workspace on the Application bar.
4 From the Workspace Switcher menu, choose **Designer Compact**	In this workspace layout, the panels are reduced to buttons on the right side of the window.

5 Click as shown	To display the Insert panel as a flyout panel.
Click the **Files** button	To display the Files panel.
Click the **Files** button again	To close it.
6 Point as shown	
Drag the Insert button above the Document toolbar	(And below the Menu bar.) To place the Insert bar.
7 From the Workspace Switcher menu, choose **Reset 'Designer Compact'**	The Insert commands switch back to the flyout panel on the right side.
8 From the Workspace Switcher menu, choose **My workspace**	To switch back to your custom workspace.
Observe the workspace	Two panel groups are displayed on the right side of the window: CSS Styles, and Files/Assets. The Insert bar is positioned above the Document toolbar and the Common tab is selected.
9 Choose **File**, **Close**	To close the index.html file.

Topic C: The Document window

This topic covers the following Adobe ACE exam objectives for Dreamweaver CS6.

#	Objective
1.1	**Working with the Document window**
1.1.1	Understanding Code view, Split view, and Design view
1.1.2	Adding a Title in the Title field (where it appears and why)
1.1.3	Difference between enabling Live View and Live Code
1.1.4	Refreshing Design view after updating code
9.4	**Understanding related files**
9.4.1	Types of related files: CSS, SSI, JavaScript, Spry data, XML.
9.4.2	Selecting related files by clicking tabs in Document window.

Document views

Explanation

Once a web page is open, you use Dreamweaver's Document window to view the page as you work on it. How the page is displayed depends on what view option is applied.

Code, Split, and Design views

There are three views in Dreamweaver that you can use to edit your design and/or the code for a web page: Code, Split, and Design. You can click the view buttons on the Document toolbar, as shown in Exhibit 1-7, to switch between the views as you work on a web page. You can also switch views by using the View menu or the Layout button in the Application bar.

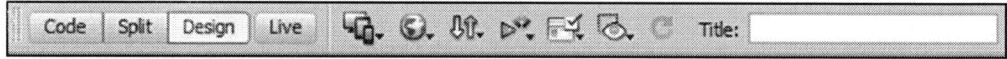

Exhibit 1-7: The Document toolbar

- **Code view** — Displays the HTML code for the web page and various code editing tools.
- **Split view** — Displays both the HTML code and the WYSIWYG editor. By default, the view is split vertically for a side-by-side display. To switch to a horizontal split, choose View, Split Vertically. To then switch the position of the Design view and Code view, choose View, Design View on Top.
- **Design view** — Displays the web page in a WYSIWYG editor, which mimics how the page would appear in a browser. This is the default view for the Designer workspace.

Do it!

C-1:   Switching the view

The files for this activity are in Student Data folder **Unit 1\Topic C**.

Here's how	Here's why
1 Start Dreamweaver CS6	If necessary.
2 Open the Harvest Valley Market Home page	Choose File, Open. Locate the current topic and double-click the index.html file in the website folder.
3 On the Document toolbar, click **Code**	To switch to Code view. Code view displays the HTML code for the web page and the coding toolbar.
4 Switch to **Split** view	To view the HTML code and the WYSIWYG editor.
5 Choose **View, Split Vertically**	To uncheck the command on the menu and change the view to a horizontal split.
6 Choose **View, Design View on Top**	To check the command on the menu and switch the position of the Design view and Code view.
7 Switch to **Design** view	

Live and Live Code views

In addition to the three traditional views, there are two other views that you can use to display the page design or code as it would appear in a browser without leaving the Dreamweaver workspace. These views are called Live view and Live Code view. You can switch to *Live view* any time you are in Design or Split view to view a non-editable version of the page. If you enter Live view while you are in Split view, the design is locked, but the code remains editable so you can change the code, and then refresh Live view to see your changes take effect.

If you are in Live view, you can also enable Live Code view. *Live Code view* is a non-editable view and displays the code that you would see if you viewed the page source from a browser.

C-2: Enabling Live and Live Code views

The files for this activity are in Student Data folder **Unit 1\Topic C**.

Here's how	Here's why
1 Click **Live**, as shown	
	To view a non-editable version of the page as it would appear in a browser.
2 Try to type on the page	To verify you cannot edit the page while in Live view.
3 Switch to Split view	The code in Code view can be edited when in Live view.
4 Click **Live Code**	
	To preview the page source code as it would appear in a browser. The code is highlighted and cannot be edited.
5 Turn off Live Code view	On the Document toolbar, click Live Code.
6 Turn off Live view	On the Document toolbar, click Live.
7 Switch to Design view	

Working in the Document window

In addition to changing the view, there are other useful features and tools you can use when working on pages in the Document window.

Document tabs

You can have multiple documents open simultaneously and switch between them by clicking the document tabs. You can also display files as floating documents so that each one appears in its own window. To open each tabbed document in a floating window, choose Window, Cascade. To return a floating window to the standard tabbed format, click the Maximize button in the upper-right corner of the window.

Related Files toolbar

Above the document view buttons is the *Related Files toolbar*, which lists all of the files to which the current page is linked such as CSS, JavaScript, XML and so on. The example in Exhibit 1-8 shows only one related file, the external style sheet globalstyles.css. The Source Code button refers to the current document. You can click any file name on the Related Files toolbar to open that file for editing. The view will switch to Split view and the related file will display in the code pane of the Document window.

Exhibit 1-8: The Related Files toolbar

Page titles

You should give every page a title. Titles are not the same as file names; titles appear in the title bar of the browser window and are used by some search engines to help provide accurate search results. To specify a page title, enter it in the Title box on the Document toolbar.

You can also enter a title in the code between the <title> tags. Whenever you add or edit the code for a page, click Refresh in the Property inspector to update the page's Design view.

Visual aids

Visual aids are page icons, symbols, or borders that are visible only in Dreamweaver to help you work precisely. You can turn individual visual aids on and off to make it easier to work with your page elements. To set your visual aids, select them from the Visual Aid list on the Document toolbar, as shown in Exhibit 1-9. To toggle all visual aids on or off, press Ctrl+Shift+I.

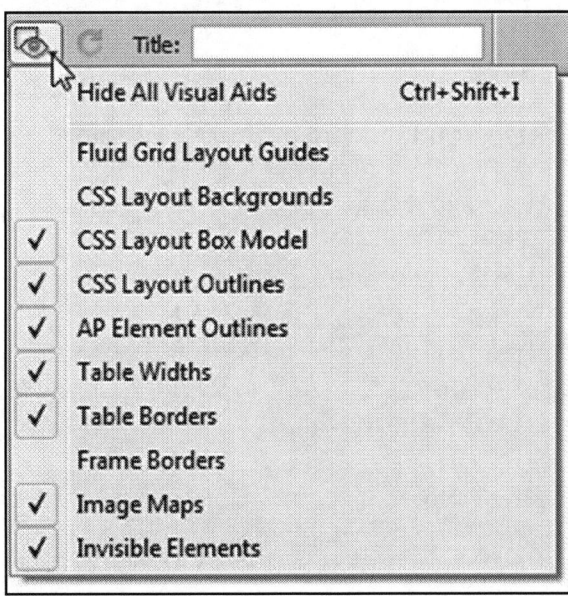

Exhibit 1-9: The Visual Aids list on the Document toolbar

The Zoom tool

The Zoom tool is the magnifying-glass icon at the bottom of the Document window in the Status bar. It allows you to quickly zoom in and out on your pages. Click anywhere on a page to zoom in, or magnify that area. To zoom out, hold down the Alt key and click the page. You can also drag a marquee around a specific area of a page to zoom in on that area, or you can enter or select a magnification value in the Set magnification box.

Do it!

C-3: Working in the Document window

The files for this activity are in Student Data folder **Unit 1\Topic C**.

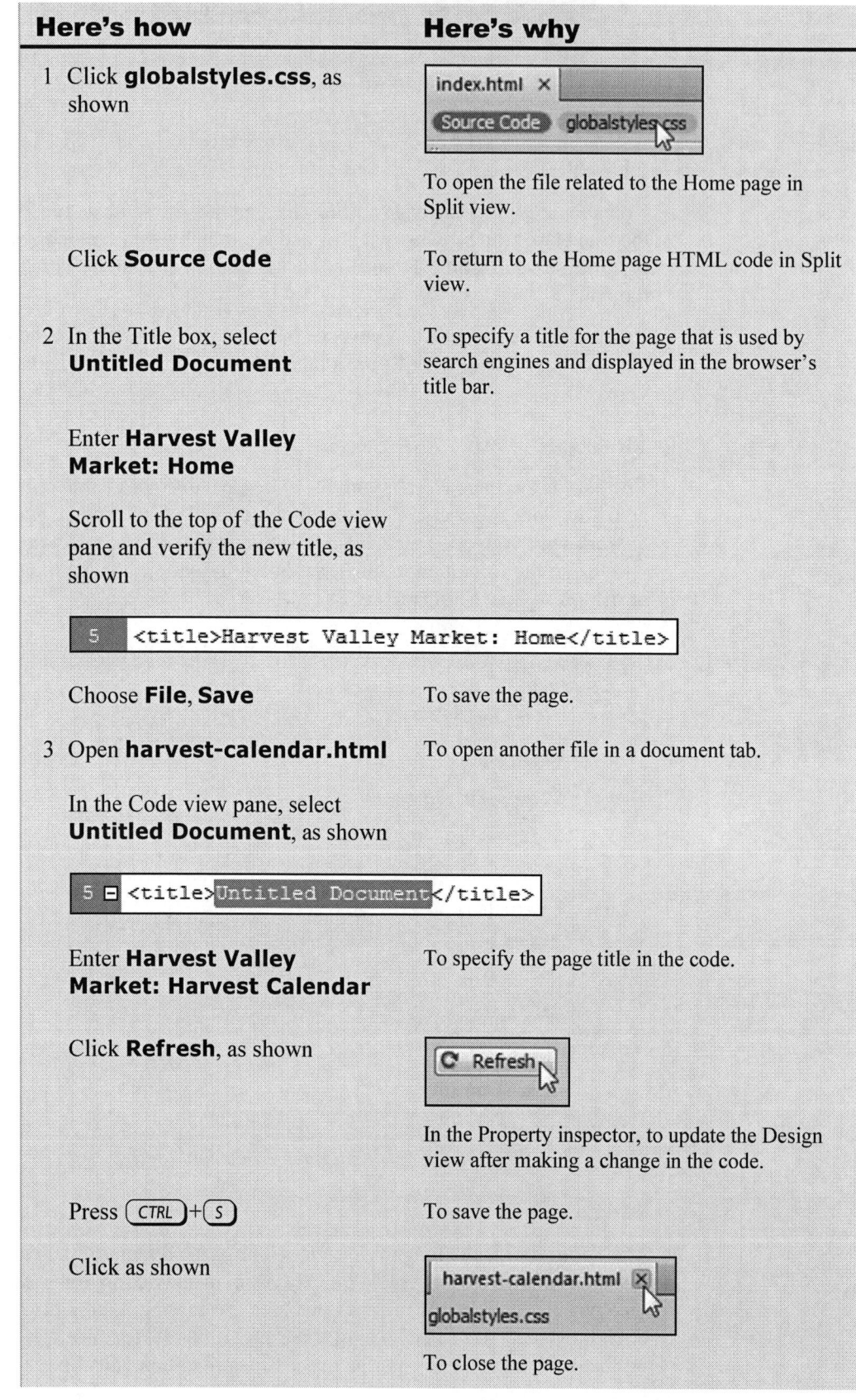

Here's how	Here's why
1 Click **globalstyles.css**, as shown	
	To open the file related to the Home page in Split view.
Click **Source Code**	To return to the Home page HTML code in Split view.
2 In the Title box, select **Untitled Document**	To specify a title for the page that is used by search engines and displayed in the browser's title bar.
Enter **Harvest Valley Market: Home**	
Scroll to the top of the Code view pane and verify the new title, as shown	
`5  <title>Harvest Valley Market: Home</title>`	
Choose **File**, **Save**	To save the page.
3 Open **harvest-calendar.html**	To open another file in a document tab.
In the Code view pane, select **Untitled Document**, as shown	
`5 ☐ <title>Untitled Document</title>`	
Enter **Harvest Valley Market: Harvest Calendar**	To specify the page title in the code.
Click **Refresh**, as shown	
	In the Property inspector, to update the Design view after making a change in the code.
Press ⌨CTRL⌨+⌨S⌨	To save the page.
Click as shown	
	To close the page.

4 Switch to Design view

5 On the Document toolbar, click   To display the Visual Aid list.

    From the list, select **CSS Layout Outlines**   To hide all CSS layout borders used in the layout. These are layout guides only; they are not displayed in a browser.

6 Show the CSS outlines again   From the Visual Aid list, select CSS Layout Outlines.

7 Click   The Zoom tool is on the Status bar at the bottom of the Document window.

    Click as shown

    To zoom in on the market image on the right side of the page.

8 Press and hold (ALT)

    Click the market image again   To zoom out.

    Release (ALT)

9 Drag a marquee over the hanging flower baskets in the image   (In the image.) To identify the zoom in location.

    Release the mouse button   To zoom in on that area of the image.

10 Click as shown

    (In the lower-right corner of the Document window.) To display the Set magnification list.

    Select **100%**   To return to the default magnification level.

11 Click   (On the Status bar at the bottom of the Document window.) The Select tool is the default tool.

Basic editing

Explanation

Adding and editing content in Design view is similar to using a word processor. Click on the page to place the insertion point, and type to insert text.

Typical page elements

Web pages can include many types of content, including text, links, images, and tables, as shown in Exhibit 1-10.

Exhibit 1-10: A sample web page

The following table describes some typical web page elements.

Element	Description
Text	Words, phrases, sentences, headings, and paragraphs.
Table	A grid structure consisting of rows and columns, meant primarily to contain tabular data, such as a product list with corresponding prices. Although tables can also help you control the layout and spacing of elements on a page, CSS is the superior method for controlling layout.
Image	A graphic file, typically in .gif, .jpg, or .png format. Images can also be used as links.
Link	Text or an image that directs the browser to another location or resource when clicked. The destination might be another web page, another area of the current page, or a file such as a PDF or Excel document.
Image map	A single graphic that can include multiple links.
Forms	Interactive pages consisting of text input fields, check boxes, and buttons that allow users to submit data to a server for processing and data storage.

Do it!   **C-4:   Discussing web page elements**

Questions and answers

1 What are links?

2 What's the difference between an image and an image map?

3 What is the best use for tables?

4 Have you ever used a form on the Internet? If so, for what purpose?

Text basics

To add text to a page, you can simply type at the insertion point, or you can copy and paste text from another source. Inserting and editing text can sometimes cause other elements on the page to move. For example, an image below a paragraph will move down as you add more text to the paragraph.

Do it!

C-5: Inserting and editing text

The files for this activity are in Student Data folder **Unit 1\Topic C**.

Here's how	Here's why
1 Verify the Harvest Valley Market Home page is open	
2 In the top paragraph, click to the left of **located**, as shown	Harvest Valley Market is |located in Springfield, to provide locally grown, fresh food to city resi
	To place the insertion point at this location.
3 Type **the largest farmers market**	To add text to the paragraph.
Press (SPACEBAR)	To add a space. This type of text editing is similar to working in a word processor.
4 Select as shown	**Today's** Specials
	The specials now last for a week instead of a single day, so you'll change "Today's" to "This Week's."
Type **This Week's**	
5 Press (CTRL) + (S)	To update the document.
Press (CTRL) + (W)	To close the index.html file.

Topic D: The Property inspector

This topic covers the following Adobe ACE exam objectives for Dreamweaver CS6.

#	Objective
1.3	**Updating properties in the Property inspector**
1.3.1	Setting contextual options to affect selected elements
1.3.2	Understanding HTML vs. CSS sections of Property inspector

Explanation

The Property inspector (also called the Properties panel) displays the options and properties of the element that's selected in the Document window. For example, if you select an image on the page, the Property inspector displays the image's properties, such as its height and width, as shown in Exhibit 1-11. You can use the Property inspector to observe properties and to set or modify properties.

Exhibit 1-11: The Property inspector, with an image selected

For example, you can select a paragraph of text and use the Property inspector to apply basic formatting such as emphasis (boldface or italics), or to assign a class or ID. You can also use the Property inspector to create links and modify tables and image maps.

When the focus is on a page element (for example, text on the page rather than embedded objects like images and videos), the Property inspector displays two buttons on the left side: HTML and CSS. By default, HTML options are displayed. Click CSS to display the CSS-related options for a selected element.

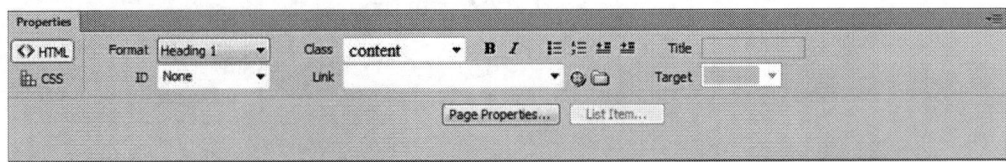

Exhibit 1-12: The Property inspector, with focus on heading text (a page element)

D-1: Working with the Property inspector

The files for this activity are in Student Data folder **Unit 1\Topic D**.

Here's how	Here's why
1 Open the Harvest Valley Market Home page	In the current topic folder.
2 On the page, drag to select **Welcome to Harvest Valley Market**	You'll use the Property inspector to view the attributes for this text.
Observe the Property inspector	It shows that this text is defined as a heading and is assigned to the content class.
3 On the left side of the Property inspector, click **CSS**	To display the CSS (Cascading Style Sheet) properties assigned to this text. The font, font size, and text color are displayed.
Click **HTML**	(On the left side of the Property inspector.) To display the HTML-related properties for the selected element. You could make the text a link and apply other basic HTML attributes.
4 Click the image shown	
	To select it.
Observe the Property inspector	It displays the attributes and options for the selected image.
5 Double-click the **Properties** tab, as shown	
	To hide the Property inspector and display more of the Document window.
Show the Property inspector again	Click the Properties tab again.
6 Scroll down to the second paragraph on the page	
Select **Rain or shine**, as shown	
Observe the Status bar	To view the tags applied to the selected text.

`<body> <div.container> <div.content> <p>`

7 In the Property inspector, click as shown

To apply emphasis (italics) to the selection.

Observe the Status bar

Dreamweaver uses the `<em>` tag to create the emphasis.

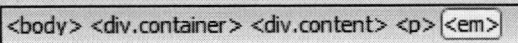

`<body> <div.container> <div.content> <p> <em>`

Click the **Italics** button again

To remove the emphasis tag.

8 Click the **Bold** button

To apply bolding to the selection. Dreamweaver uses the `<strong>` tag to create the bolding.

9 Click **Specials**

To place the insertion point in the heading "This Week's Specials."

Click **CSS**

(In the Property inspector.) To display the style properties of the selected element. With this option selected, styles that you apply will be created in the style sheet rather than using HTML tags.

10 Click in the Size box, as shown

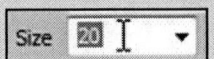

To select the heading size value.

Type **22**

To change the heading size to 22 pixels.

Press `↵ ENTER`

To apply the size change. Notice that the change was applied to the entire heading not just the "Specials" text.

11 Press `CTRL`+`S`

To save your changes to index.html.

In the Related Files toolbar, click as shown

To open the globalstyles.css file in Split view. Notice the filename has an asterisk next to it indicating changes were made and the file has not been saved with those changes.

Press `CTRL`+`S`

To save your changes in the style sheet.

12 Choose **File**, **Close**

To close the index.html file.

Topic E: Previewing a web page

This topic covers the following Adobe ACE exam objectives for Dreamweaver CS6.

#	Objective
3.3	Previewing pages in a browser
3.3.1	Setting the primary and secondary browsers
3.3.2	Understanding the advantages of testing pages in a browser

Testing pages in a browser

Explanation

As you work on a page, you'll probably want to periodically see it as it will appear in a browser. To preview a web page in a browser:

1 On the Document toolbar, click the Preview/Debug in browser button.

2 From the drop-down list, select a browser.

3 If you have not yet saved your changes, a dialog box opens, prompting you to save your changes. Click Yes to save your changes and preview the page in the selected browser.

Do it!

E-1: Previewing a page in a browser

The files for this activity are in Student Data folder **Unit 1\Topic E**.

Here's how	Here's why
1 Open the Harvest Valley Market Home page	In the current topic folder.
2 On the Document toolbar, click 🌐	(The Preview/Debug in browser button.) To display a list of options.
3 Select **Preview in Firefox**	To view the page in Firefox.
4 Close the browser	

Adding browsers to the Preview list

Explanation

Not all browsers display a web page the same way—there are often minor differences in how each browser interprets HTML and CSS code, and these differences can affect the way a page looks and functions. What looks good in one browser might not look good in another. For this reason, it's a good idea to preview your web pages in several popular browsers. This practice will help you to tweak the page so that it looks and functions as you intended in multiple browsers.

When you first install Dreamweaver, it detects the browsers installed on your computer. It uses your default browser as the primary browser for previewing pages. You can add other browsers as needed.

To add other browsers to the Preview list:

1 On the Document toolbar, click the Preview/Debug in browser button and choose Edit Browser List to open the Preferences dialog box. (You can also choose Edit, Preferences or press Ctrl+U to open the Preferences dialog box.)

2 In the Category list, select Preview in Browser.

3 Click the plus sign next to Browsers to open the Add Browser dialog box.

4 In the Name box, type a name for the browser.

5 Click the Browse button, and navigate to the .exe file for the desired browser (typically located in a folder in the C:\Program Files folder).

6 Check Secondary browser.

7 Click OK to close the Add Browser dialog box.

8 Repeat steps 3–7 for each browser you want to add to the preview menu.

9 Click OK to close the Preferences dialog box.

Do it!

E-2:   Setting the primary and secondary browsers

The files for this activity are in Student Data folder **Unit 1\Topic E**.

Here's how	Here's why
1 Click 🌐.	The Preview/Debug in browser button on the Document toolbar.
Choose **Edit Browser List...**	
2 In the Category list, select **Preview in Browser**	If necessary.
3 In the Browsers box, select **Firefox**	If Firefox is set as the default browser the Primary browser box will be checked.
Check the **Primary browser** box	If Firefox is not the default browser. To set Firefox as the primary browser.
4 In the Browsers box, select **IExplore**	
Check **Secondary browser**	To set Internet Explorer as the secondary browser.
5 Click **OK**	To close the Preferences dialog box.
6 Click 🌐.	
Select **Preview in IExplore**	To view the Home page in Internet Explorer.
Click **No**	If Internet Explorer asks you to make it the default browser.
7 Close the browser	
Close index.html	

Unit summary: Getting started

Topic A   In this topic, you learned about the Internet, the Web, and HTML. You learned that HTML and XHTML are standard markup languages used to build web pages, and that Dreamweaver uses XHTML code by default.

Topic B   In this topic, you identified the main components of the **Dreamweaver CS6 workspace**. You learned how to switch between the predefined **workspace layouts**. Then, you learned how to adjust **panels** in the Document window and create a custom workspace.

Topic C   In this topic, you learned how to switch **views** in the Document window and the differences between the five Dreamweaver views: **Code**, **Split**, **Design**, **Live**, and **Live Code**. You learned the features and tools available while you work in the Document window. You also performed some basic **text editing**.

Topic D   In this topic, you learned how to update page element properties and embedded object properties using the **Property inspector**. You also learned how to switch between the HTML and CSS sections of the Property inspector when the focus is on a page element.

Topic E   In this topic, you learned how to **preview** a page in a browser. You also learned how to set the primary and secondary preview browsers.

Independent practice activity

In this activity, you'll insert a page title, apply basic text formatting, and preview the page in Firefox.

The files for this activity are in Student Data folder **Unit 1\Unit summary**.

1 Open **history.html**.

2 Specify the page title **Harvest Valley Market: History**.
 (*Hint:* In the Title box on the Document toolbar.)

3 Drag to select the text **What's good for you is good for your community**.
 (*Hint:* Text is located at the bottom of the page, last sentence on the white background.)

4 Using the Property inspector, make the text bold.
 (*Hint:* View the HTML options and then click the Bold button.)

5 Save the page and preview it in Firefox.

6 Close the browser to return to Dreamweaver.

7 Close all open files.

Review questions

1 Dreamweaver CS6 builds web pages with _____ code by default.

2 The _____ window displays the current page. This is where you'll do most of your work.

3 How do you convert the Insert panel to the Insert bar?

4 True or False: You can rename or delete custom workspaces by choosing Manage Workspaces from the Workspace Switcher menu.

5 True or False: If you enter Live view from Split view, the content is editable but the code is not.

6 Above the document view buttons is the _____ toolbar, which lists all of the files to which the current page is linked.

7 You can use tables to layout a web page, but _____ is the superior method for controlling page layout.

8 True or false? The properties and options that are displayed in the Property inspector changed based on what is selected in the Document window.

9 The keyboard shortcut for previewing a webpage in the primary browser is _____.

10 The keyboard shortcut for previewing a web page in the secondary browser is _____.

Unit 2

Websites and pages

Complete this unit, and you'll know how to:

A Use flowchart and wireframe tools to plan your site before building it.

B Define a local site and local root folder to store the website while development is in progress.

C Create new web pages and set the default document type and page extension.

D Use the Files panel to sort files and choose and manage sites.

E Use the Files panel to organize site files and folders to assist in mapping the site and to keep links intact.

Topic A: Planning a website

Explanation

You've already explored basic site planning concepts. Next you'll learn about some common planning and organizational tools and methods you can apply to plan your site before you start building it. Organizing site files in a logical structure is a critical part of this process. A good site structure makes it easier to maintain the site efficiently over time.

Think about how best to structure your pages and content, how you want to present information, and how you want the site to look (color schemes, fonts, and so on) before you begin the actual work. Because content requirements, design changes, and job assignments typically change over time, you should plan and design a site that is easy to maintain and easy to transfer to another developer or team of developers.

Planning tools

Flowcharts and wireframes are effective planning tools that you can use individually or with a group to help map out and visualize your site plan.

Flowcharts

A well-designed site must have an effective navigation scheme. You need to plan the link relationships between the pages in your site. Sometimes you can prevent problems by drafting a site flowchart, similar to the simple example shown in Exhibit 2-1.

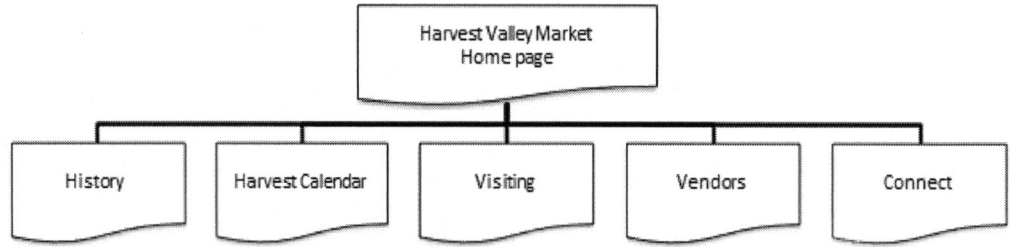

Exhibit 2-1: A simple flowchart for the Harvest Valley Market site

Keeping a flowchart up-to-date as you build your site can also help you create a site map when you're ready to publish the site. A *site map* is like a table of contents for a site. It should provide the visitor with links to the main topics or sections in the site and reveal the site's content hierarchy. In this way, site maps enhance the usability of a site, especially if the site is complex or contains a lot of information.

Wireframes

A wireframe is similar to a flowchart in that it provides a visual guide for the creation of a website, showing link relationships between pages and the general hierarchy of information. However, a wireframe is more of a design mockup—a template that shows the placement of page elements like logos, navigation bars, major content sections, and so on. Wireframes act as a sort of skeleton for a site and help you maintain design consistency across all site pages.

You can create multiple wireframes depicting layout and design variations, enabling participants to brainstorm ideas and offer suggestions. Wireframes help you visualize what the finished product will look like so that you and/or the project team can review and critique it before the bulk of the work is done. Adobe Fireworks is a popular software tool for creating wireframes, as well as site graphics and actual pages.

Do it!

A-1:   Discussing planning tools

Here's how	Here's why
1 How can creating a flowchart help you build a site?	
2 How might using wireframes help you build and optimize a site layout?	
3 Open Firefox	
4 In the Address bar, type **http://www.nasa.gov**	
Press (↵ ENTER)	To go to the NASA site.
5 Click **Missions**	
Click **Current Missions**	
Observe how the information is structured	
6 Do you think the site structures information in a logical and effective hierarchy? Why or why not?	
7 Close Firefox	

Topic B: Setting up a site

This topic covers the following Adobe ACE exam objectives for Dreamweaver CS6.

#	Objective
2.1	**Creating the local root folder**
2.1.1	Understanding the concept of the site's local root folder

Local, remote, and testing sites

Explanation

When you get started on a site, you'll set up a local site folder in which to build your site files. You might also need to establish a testing folder on a web server if your site includes applications that interact with data. When you're ready to publish your site, you'll upload it to a remote server.

The following table describes local, remote, and testing sites.

Folder	Location	Purpose
Local	Your local hard disk	To store work in progress. You can transfer files from the local site to the other sites when they're complete.
Remote	The web server where your site is published	To make your site available to your intended audience.
Testing	Any computer running the server and application software you need	To test your connection to databases and dynamic pages (pages that change according to information received from databases or page variables).

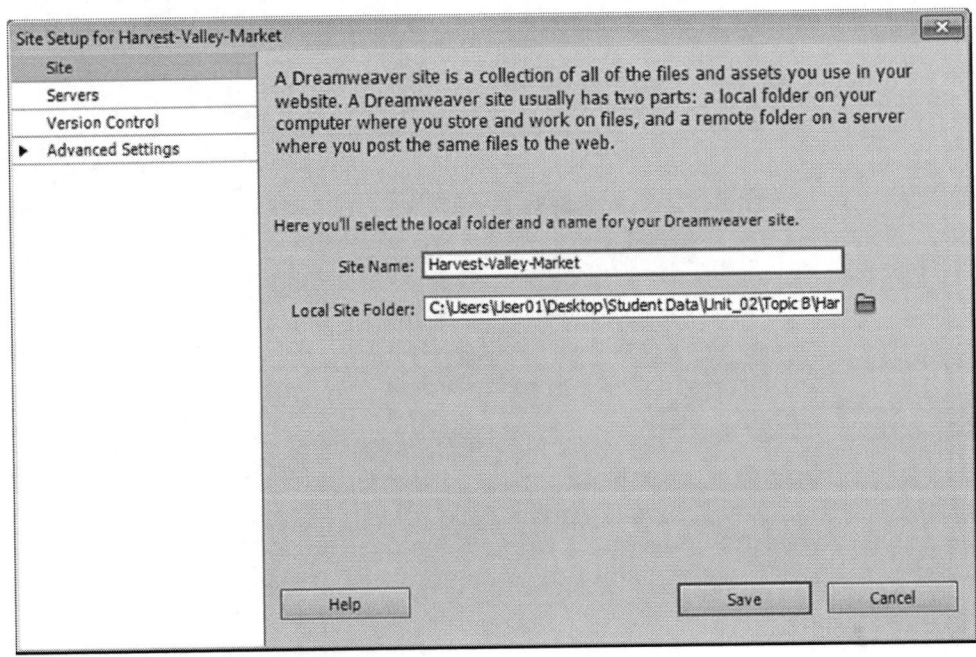

Exhibit 2-2: The Site Setup dialog box

Defining a local site

The local folder on your computer is where you work on the site before publishing it on the Internet. After you verify that it looks and functions as you intend, you can publish it to a remote folder on the web server that hosts your site.

A local site serves as the root folder for your website. (The local *root folder* is at the top of the site hierarchy; it contains all other site folders and files.) Any folder on your computer—except your hard drive root directory (C:\) or the Dreamweaver application folder—can serve as the local site folder.

To define a local site:

1   Choose Site, New Site to open the Site Setup dialog box, shown in Exhibit 2-2.

2   In the Site name box, enter a name for the site.

3   In the Local Site Folder box, enter the path to the folder or click the folder icon to browse to and select the folder.

4   Click Save. The site files and folders are displayed in the Files panel.

Do it!

B-1:   Defining a local site

The files for this activity are in Student Data folder **Unit 2\Topic B**.

Here's how	Here's why
1 Choose **Site, New Site...**	To open the Site Setup dialog box.
2 In the Site Name box, type **Harvest-Valley-Market**	To name the site.
Click as shown	**Browse for folder**
	To open the Choose Root Folder dialog box where you can browse to locate the site folder.
3 Click **Desktop**	On the left side of the dialog box.
Open the Student Data folder	
Open the current unit folder	
4 In the current topic folder, open the **Harvest Valley Market** folder	
Click **Select**	To set the root folder for this site, where the files for the site will be stored.
Click **Save**	To define the root site folder.
5 Observe the Files panel	Harvest-Valley-Market is the site name, but right now it doesn't contain any folders or files.

Topic C: Creating web pages

This topic covers the following Adobe ACE exam objectives for Dreamweaver CS6.

#	Objective
3.1	**Using the New Document dialog box**
3.1.1	Describing the basic file types Dreamweaver can create
3.1.2	Setting the default page extension preference (.html or .htm)
6.1	**Understanding basic CSS syntax**
6.1.6	Understanding the difference between margin and padding
6.1.7	Setting color properties with hexadecimal values

New Document dialog box

Explanation

You can work with a variety of file types in Dreamweaver. The primary kind of file you will work with is the HTML file. You can create new files of various types using the New Document dialog box. Some of the other common file types you might use when working in Dreamweaver include:

- **CSS** (Cascading Style Sheets) files have a .css extension. They are used to format HTML content and control the positioning of various page elements.

- **JavaScript** have a .js extension. JavaScript is a scripting language used to make web pages interactive.

- **XML** (Extensible Markup Language) files have a .xml extension. They contain data in a raw form that can be formatted using XSL (Extensible Stylesheet Language).

- **CFML** (ColdFusion Markup Language) files have a .cfm extension and are used to process dynamic pages.

- **PHP** (Hypertext Preprocessor) files have a .php extension and are also used to process dynamic pages.

To create a web page, choose File, New. This opens the New Document dialog box, as shown in Exhibit 2-3.

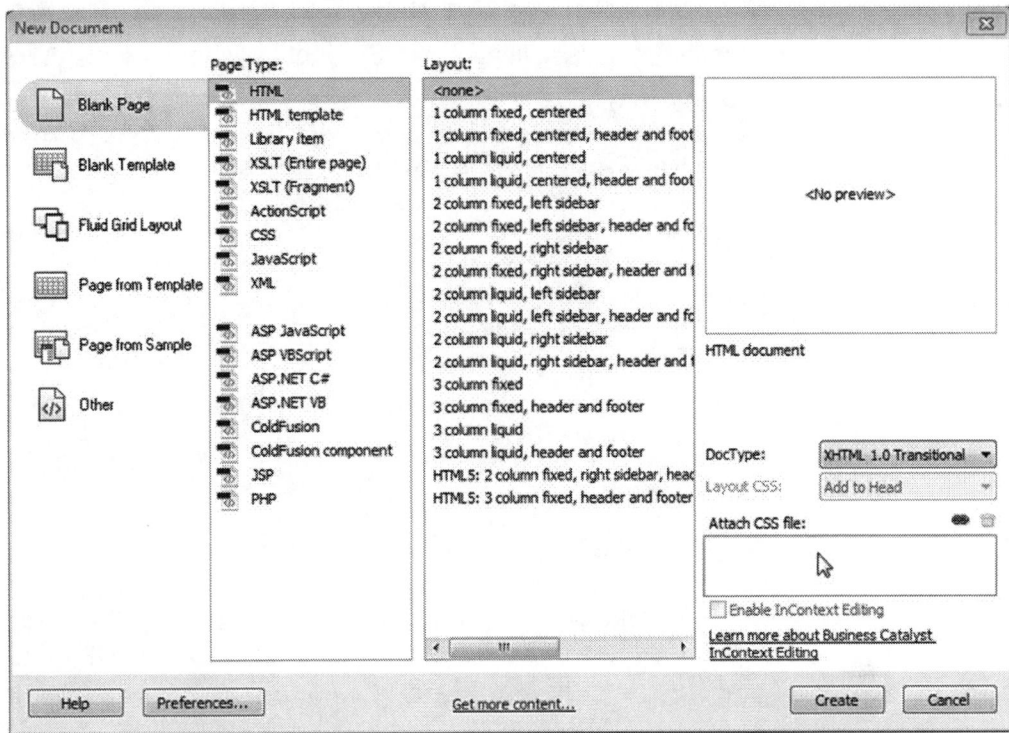

Exhibit 2-3: The New Document dialog box

The New Document dialog box has several options, described in the following table.

Option	Description
Blank Page	You can create a new, blank HTML page that contains only the basic document tag structure with no content. You can also create a blank page that contains "dummy" content in a preset layout that you can modify to suit your needs. Using the Blank Page category of the New Document dialog box, you can also create CSS documents, XML documents, and many other types of documents.
Blank Template	This set of options provides HTML templates, plus templates for server technologies such as ASP.NET and ColdFusion. These templates are attached to predefined CSS style sheets, which provide a layout framework that you can build on.
Fluid Grid Layout	This is a system for designing websites that adapt to various devices such as mobile phones, tablets, and desktop computers. By default, Dreamweaver creates three layouts with different numbers of columns and resolution widths and the DocType is HTML5.
Page from Template	This option shows a list of your own templates from which you can create pages.
Page from Sample	This option provides several basic style sheets that you can use and modify.

Do it!   ### C-1:   Exploring the New Document dialog box

The files for this activity are in Student Data folder **Unit 2\Topic C**.

Here's how	Here's why
1 Choose **Site, Manage Sites...**	To open the Manage Sites dialog box.
Double-click **Harvest-Valley-Market**	To open the Site Setup dialog box.
Click the browse button	(To the right of the Local Site Folder text box.) The Choose Root Folder dialog box is displayed.
Browse to the Harvest Valley Market folder	In the current topic folder.
Click **Select**	To update the location of the local site files.
Click **Save**	If necessary, click OK to recreate the cache.
Click **Done**	
2 Choose **File, New...**	To open the New Document dialog box as shown in Exhibit 2-3.
Verify that **Blank Page** is selected	**New Document** Blank Page
Verify that **HTML** and **<none>** are selected	Page Type: Layout: HTML <none>
	In the Page Type list and the Layout list, respectively. The default page is an HTML page without a layout. Observe the other types of files that Dreamweaver can create.
3 Select **Blank Template**	The middle column is now types of templates.
4 Select **Fluid Grid Layout**	To view the settings for the three default adaptive layouts.

5	Select **Page from Sample**	To view a variety of sample CSS style sheets.
	Verify **CSS Style Sheet** is selected	In the Sample Folder list.
	Select **Full Design: Arial, Blue/Green/Gray**	In the Sample Page list.
	Observe the preview	The preview in the top, right corner displays a sample of the CSS styles that would be included in this style sheet.
6	Switch between the layouts	To observe other starter style sheets.
7	Click **Cancel**	To close the New Document dialog box.

Creating a web page

Explanation

Dreamweaver provides several options for creating web pages. You can create pages from scratch, or you can use layout templates. Depending on the nature of your site and your own development preferences, you might choose to start from scratch, or you might prefer to have some of the work done for you before you get started.

Creating a web page from scratch

To create a blank HTML page:

1 Choose File, New to open the New Document dialog box.
(You can also press Ctrl+N.)
2 Select Blank Page (if necessary).
3 In the Page Type list, verify that HTML is selected (at the top of the list).
4 In the Layout list, verify that <none> is selected, and then click Create.

Creating a web page from a predefined layout

The layout templates provided by Dreamweaver are a good starting point. Choose the layout that best fits your wireframe design. To create a web page from a layout template:

1 Choose File, New.
2 Select Blank Page (if necessary).
3 In the Page Type list, verify that HTML is selected.
4 In the Layout list, select the layout closest to your wireframe design, and then click Create.

File names and file extensions

The file name you choose for your home page is important. Home pages are usually named index.html or default.html because web servers are typically configured to look for that file name as the website's *root*, or top-level file. File names cannot include special characters such as (, $, #, @ and &, and cannot contain spaces. You can use underscore characters if you want to separate words or letters.

When you save a new web page, it's important that you name it with the appropriate file extension, such as .htm or .html. If applicable, check with your server administrator to verify the naming conventions in use in your organization. You might also need to save pages with file extensions for specific application processing, such as .asp for an Active Server Pages document or .cfm for a ColdFusion document.

To set the default document type and page extension:

1 Choose Edit, Preferences to open the Preferences dialog box.

2 From the Category list, select New Document.

3 From the Default document list, select the type of document you want to open by default.

4 In the Default extension list, modify the extension as needed. For example, change .html to .htm for an HTML page.

5 Click OK.

Do it!

C-2: Creating a new web page

The files for this activity are in Student Data folder **Unit 2\Topic C**.

Here's how	Here's why
1 Choose **Edit**, **Preferences...**	To open the Preferences dialog box.
2 Select **New Document**	In the Category list.
3 In the Default document list, verify **HTML** is selected	Default document: HTML Default extension: .html
Verify **.html** is the default extension	
4 Click **OK**	To close the Preferences dialog box.
5 Choose **File, New...**	To open the New Document dialog box.
Verify that **Blank Page** is selected	
Verify that **HTML** and **<none>** are selected	In the Page Type list and the Layout list, respectively.
Click **Create**	To open a blank HTML page. Notice this page does not contain any layout formatting.

6   Click as shown

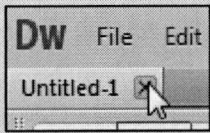

To close the blank page without saving it.

7   Choose **File**, **New...**

Verify that **HTML** is selected   In the Page Type list.

Select **1 column fixed,**   In the Layout list.
centered, header and
footer

Click **Create**   To create a page based on a predefined layout.
                                        This layout has one column for the web page
                                        content as well as a header and footer.

8   Enter **Harvest Valley**   In the Document toolbar Title box.
    Market: Home as the page title

9   Select **Instructions**

    Type **Welcome to Harvest**
    Valley Market

10 Choose **File**, **Save**   (Or press Ctrl+S.) The Save As dialog box
                                        appears because this is a new document that
                                        hasn't been saved yet.

    Edit the File name box to read
    index.html

    Click **Save**

11 Verify that index.html appears in
    the Files panel list

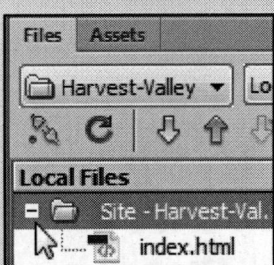

12 Close index.html

Page properties

Explanation

With the Page Properties dialog box, you can set basic page design options, such as the font, font size, and background color. To open the Page Properties dialog box:

- Click the Page Properties button in the Property inspector
- Choose Modify, Page Properties
- Press Ctrl+J

When you use the Page Properties dialog box to apply styles, they will be applied to the current page only. When you want multiple pages to share the same styles, you need to use a style sheet.

Page margins

A *page margin* is the space between the content on a page and the edges of the browser window. (Margins may also exist between individual elements.) Browsers apply their own default page margins, typically between 10 and 15 pixels of space on all four sides. It's important that you set your own page margins to ensure that they are consistent in different browsers.

You can also set your page margins to zero so that some of your content, such as a navigation bar or header logo, can appear flush with the edge of the browser window. You can then apply margins to large content sections or individual elements to ensure that other content is offset from the browser window's edge and other page elements.

Background color

By default, web pages have a white background, but you can apply any background color. To do so, select a color from the Background color box in the Page Properties dialog box. Clicking the Background color box opens a *color picker*—a palette with a set of color swatches, as shown in Exhibit 2-4. By default, the color picker displays the web safe colors, a standard set of 216 colors supported consistently by various operating systems. However, you are not limited to these colors and can use the picker to select just about any color you want. Web safe colors are a throwback to days when monitors only supporting limited colors and this is not an issue with modern monitors, tablets, and mobile devices.

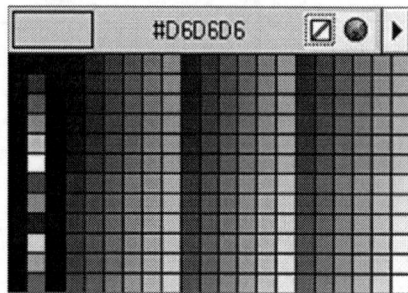

Exhibit 2-4: The color picker

Setting a default text color

Text is black by default. You can change the color of text that you select on a page, or you can set a default color for all text on a page by using the Page Properties dialog box. You might want to do this if your website uses a colored background that makes black text difficult to read or if you just want to establish a complementary color scheme.

Whenever you apply text colors and background colors, you should make sure that there's sufficient contrast between them to allow for easy reading. Insufficient contrast can strain the eyes and make reading difficult.

Hexadecimal color values

When you point to a color swatch, a three- or six-digit hexadecimal code for the color appears at the top of the color picker. Computer monitors use combinations of red, green, and blue to create the colors you see, and the hexadecimal scheme specifies combinations of those colors: the first two characters represent the intensity of red, the next two of green, and the last two of blue.

Hexadecimal notation uses the scale 0123456789ABCDEF, with 0 (zero) representing almost no color and F representing 15 times the intensity of 0. Hexadecimal values always start with the pound sign (#). The code #000000 (the lowest level of red, green, and blue) represents black, while #FFFFFF (the fullest intensity of red, green, and blue) represents white. To create yellow, you would add red and green, but no blue, so the hex code would be #FFFF00.

Hexadecimal codes that consist of only three values, such as #FFF or #3BA, are shortcuts for value pairs. The full values would be #FFFFFF and #33BBAA, respectively. Color values that do not consist of three matching pairs, such as #4BC9AE, cannot be reduced in this way.

Do it!

C-3: Setting up page properties

The files for this activity are in Student Data folder **Unit 2\Topic C**.

Here's how	Here's why
1 Open a blank HTML page with no layout	Choose File, New, then select HTML as the page type and <none> as the layout.
2 Switch to **Split** view	(If necessary.) To view both the design and code for the page.
3 Click as shown	With the HMTL option selected in the Property inspector, display the Format list.
Select **Paragraph**	To create the paragraph tags for some text.
Place the insertion point at the top of the page	If necessary.
Type **Welcome to Harvest Valley Market**	In the Design pane.

4 In the Property inspector, click the **Page Properties** button	To open the Page Properties dialog box. You'll set basic style attributes for the current page.
In the Category list, select **Appearance (HTML)**	You will apply styles by using HTML attributes.
5 Click the Background color box	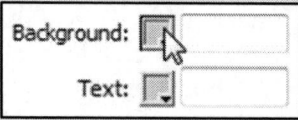
	A color picker appears. The pointer changes to an eyedropper.
Click as shown	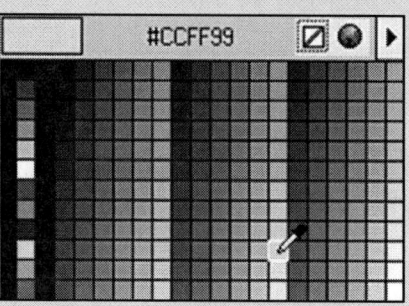
	(In the bottom-right corner.) To apply a pale green color.
6 Click the Text color box	To open the color picker.
Select the color #006600	#006600
	To select a dark green color for the text.
Click **Apply**	To apply the changes without closing the dialog box. The page now has a pale green background and the text is dark green.
7 In the Left margin box, enter **20**	To give the page a left margin of 20 pixels.
8 In the three other margin boxes, enter **20**	To set the margin to 20 pixels on all four sides of the page.
Click **OK**	To apply the changes and close the Page Properties dialog box. Notice that there is now slightly more space between the text and the edges of the page.
9 Observe the Code pane	```<body bgcolor="#CCFF99" text= "#006600" leftmargin="20" topmargin= "20" marginwidth="20" marginheight= "20">```

10 Save the file as **properties-html.html**   Press Ctrl+S or choose File, Save.

Close the file

11 Open a new blank HTML page with no layout.

12 Enter **Welcome to Harvest Valley Market** in a paragraph

13 Click **Page Properties**   In the Property inspector. You will apply styles by using CSS (Cascading Style Sheets), instead of HTML attributes.

In the Category list, select **Appearance (CSS)**   If necessary.

14 Set the Text color to **#060**   Using the color picker, or you can type the color codes into the text box.

15 Set the Background to **#CF9**

16 Enter **20** in each of the margin boxes

17 Click **OK**   Notice the page looks the same as before.

18 Observe the Code pane

```
<style type="text/css">
body,td,th {
    color: #060;
}
body {
    background-color: #CF9;
    margin-left: 20px;
    margin-top: 20px;
    margin-right: 20px;
    margin-bottom: 20px;
}
</style>
```

The styles are no longer on the body tag; instead they are now in between style tags.

19 Save the page as **properties-css.html**

Close the page

Topic D: Exploring website files

This topic covers the following Adobe ACE exam objectives for Dreamweaver CS6.

#	Objective
1.2	**Managing files in the Files panel**
1.2.1	Understanding how to configure Files panel to sort files
1.2.2	Using the options in the Files panel to choose/manage sites

The Files panel

Explanation

After you define a site, the site files are displayed in the Files panel, along with any subfolders that exist in your local root site folder. To switch to a different site, click the Site menu and choose a site. You can also access files, folders, and drives that are not part of your Dreamweaver sites from the Site menu. To make changes to a site's settings, choose Manage Sites and double-click the site to display the Site Setup dialog box.

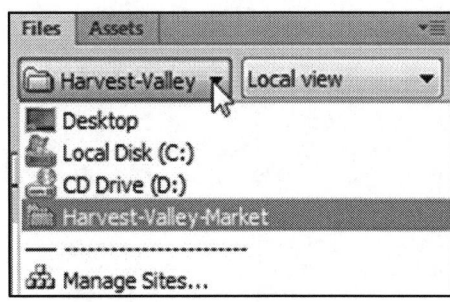

Exhibit 2-5: The Site menu

Sorting files

To sort files in the Files panel, click the heading for the column you want to sort. You can add, delete or change the order of columns that appear in the Files panel:

1 Choose Site, Manage Sites.

2 Double-click the site.

3 Expand Advanced Settings and select File View Columns and do any of the following:

   • Select a column and click the Plus (+) button to add a column.

   • Select a column and click the Minus (-) button to delete a column.

   • Select a column and click the up or down arrow button to change the position of the column. The Name column cannot be moved.

4 Click Save and Done to close the dialog boxes.

Do it!

D-1: Examining the Files panel

The files for this activity are in Student Data folder **Unit 2\Topic D**.

Here's how	Here's why
1 Click the Site menu, as shown	Files Assets ☐ Harvest-Valley ▾ Lo⸢ 🖳 Desktop 💾 Local Disk (C:) 💿 CD Drive (D:) 📁 Harvest-Valley-Market ——— ····················· 🔲 Manage Sites...
Choose **Manage Sites...**	To open the Manage Sites dialog box.
2 Double-click **Harvest-Valley-Market**	To open the Site Setup dialog box and update the site to the current topic.
Locate and select the Harvest Valley Market folder in the current topic	
Click **Save**, and then click **Done**	To close the Site Setup and Manage Sites dialog boxes.
3 Click as shown	**Local Files** ⊞ ☐ Site - Harvest-Valley-Market
	In the Files panel to expand the site.
4 Drag the left edge of the Files panel to make it wider	To view the column headings. By default the headings are Local Files, Size, Type, Modified, and Checked Out By.
5 Click **Local Files**	To sort the files by their file names.
Click **Size**	To sort the files by their sizes.
6 Open the Manage Sites dialog box	In the Files panel, click the Site menu and choose Manage Sites.
Open the Site Setup for Harvest-Valley-Market	Double-click Harvest-Valley-Market. You are going to change the available columns.

7 Click **Advanced Settings**

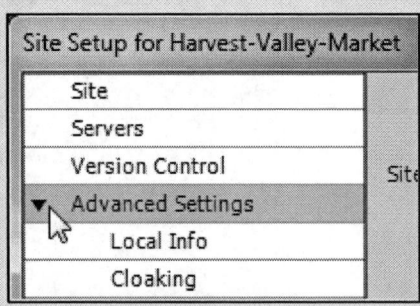

To expand the list of advanced settings.

    Click **File View Columns**

8 Click **Notes**

Notice this column is hidden.

    Click as shown 4 times

Name	Type	Show
Name	Built In	Show
Notes	Built In	Hide
Size	Built In	Show
Type	Built In	Show
Modified	Built In	Show
Checked Out By	Built In	Show

To move the Notes column to the bottom of list.

9 Double-click **Checked Out By**

    Clear the **Show** box

To hide the Checked Out By column.

    Click **Save**

10 Click **Save**, and then click **Done**

To close the Site Setup and Manage Sites dialog boxes.

11 Verify the Checked Out By column is now hidden

12 Resize and observe the Files panel

Notice that the Checked Out By column is no longer displayed.

    Resize the Panels Group

To display more of the Document window.

Topic E: Managing site files

This topic covers the following Adobe ACE exam objectives for Dreamweaver CS6.

#	Objective
3.2	**Creating and managing files with the Files panel**
3.2.1	Understanding why pages must be saved in local root folder
3.2.2	Organizing the hierarchy of files/folders to create site map
3.2.3	Repositioning pages in the Files panel prevents broken links

Organizing site files

Explanation

You should keep all the files you plan to use in the site in a logical, organized folder structure. For example, Exhibit 2-6 shows a typical folder structure for a simple website. All images are stored in their own folder. You might also have separate folders to store resources such as style sheets, PDF files, videos, and scripts.

If you save a file in a folder outside of the local root, it will be hard to maintain the site's structure when you transfer the site to a web server.

Dreamweaver does not create this structure for you when you define a site—you need to organize your files and folders inside your site's local root folder. The organization of your files in the local root folder on the local machine should map directly to the remote folder on the web server. Creating a structure that maps to your remote folder makes it easier to create a site map.

Exhibit 2-6: The Files panel, showing a folder structure for a simple site

Files and folders

You can also create new folders and HTML files directly within the Files panel and then move them as needed. In addition to creating new files and folders, you can also open files, rename files and folders, and delete files and folders:

- To open a file from the Files panel, double-click the file.
- To delete a file from the Files panel (and therefore from the site), select the file, press Delete, and then click Yes to confirm the deletion.
- To rename a file, click it twice slowly to select the file name; then type the new file name and press Enter.

If you move a file into or out of a folder using the Files panel, Dreamweaver updates all relevant links automatically. This can help to prevent broken links in your site.

Do it!

E-1: Organizing site files

The files for this activity are in Student Data folder **Unit 2\Topic E**.

Here's how	Here's why
1 Open the Site Setup for Harvest-Valley-Market dialog box	Display the Manage Sites dialog box and then double-click Harvest-Valley-Market.
2 Update the location of the Local Site Folder to the current unit and topic	Click the browse button, and then locate and select the current unit and topic.
3 Observe the file and folder structure	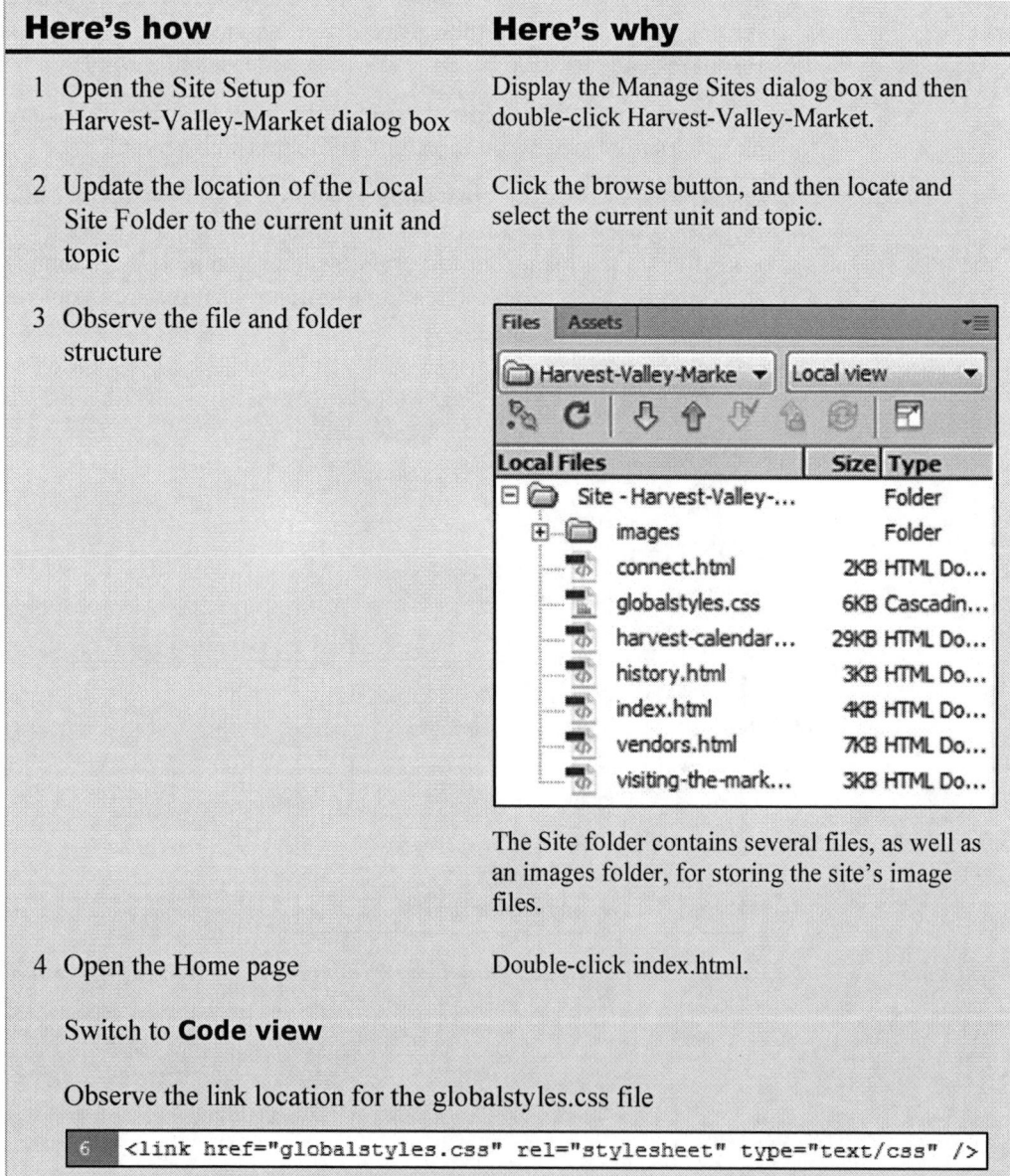
	The Site folder contains several files, as well as an images folder, for storing the site's image files.
4 Open the Home page	Double-click index.html.
Switch to **Code view**	
Observe the link location for the globalstyles.css file	

```
6   <link href="globalstyles.css" rel="stylesheet" type="text/css" />
```

5 Click as shown

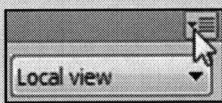

To display the Files panel menu.

Choose **File**

Choose **New Folder**   To create a new folder.

Enter **css** and press (↵ ENTER)   To name the folder. You'll store your cascading style sheets in this folder.

6 Drag the **globalstyles.css** file into   When you release the mouse, the Update Files
   the css folder   dialog opens. If you are prompted to scan for
                                                 files, click Scan.

7 Click **Update**   To update the links to the style sheet in the web
                                                 pages.

8 Click in a blank code area for the
   Home page

Verify the link location has changed

```
6   <link href="css/globalstyles.css" rel="stylesheet" type="text/css" />
```

Save and close the Home page

Unit summary: Websites and pages

Topic A   In this topic, you learned how to use **planning tools** such as **flowcharts** and **wireframes** to plan a website before you start building it.

Topic B   In this topic, you learned how to define a **local site** and set the **local root folder** where a website is stored while development is in progress.

Topic C   In this topic, you learned how to create a new web page using the **New Documents** dialog box. You learned there are a variety of page types you can choose between when creating a new web page such as **HTML**, **PHP**, **CSS**, and **JavaScript**. You also learned how to set the default document type and page extension.

Topic D   In this topic, you learned how to use the **Files panel** to **sort** files, select a site, and manage **site setup** information.

Topic E   In this topic, you learned how to use the Files panel to **organize site files** and folders to create a logical structure that can be used to create a **site map**. You also learned that when a site file is repositioned in the Files panel the links are automatically updated.

Independent practice activity

In this activity, you'll define a new website, add pages and folders to it, and change the background color of a page.

The files for this activity are in Student Data folder **Unit 2\Unit summary**.

1 Define a new site named **Practice-Harvest-Valley-Market**.
   (*Hint:* In the Manage Sites dialog box, click New Site to get started. Make sure to name the site **Practice-Harvest-Valley-Market** and navigate to the correct folder in the current unit summary folder.)

2 Create six blank HTML pages with no layout that use these file names and page titles:

File name	Page title
connect.html	Harvest Valley Market: Connect
home.html	Harvest Valley Market: Home
history.html	Harvest Valley Market: History
harvest-calendar.html	Harvest Valley Market: Calendar
visiting.html	Harvest Valley Market: Visiting
vendors.html	Harvest Valley Market: Vendors

3 On the **history.html** page, modify the HTML attributes to change the background color to a yellow color.
   (*Hint:* In the Page Properties dialog box, select the Appearance (HTML) category and click the Background color box to select a shade of yellow.)

4 Add two folders to the site named **css** and **images**.

5 Save and close all open pages.

Review questions

1 True or False: The purpose of your local site is to make it available to your intended audience.

2 To create a new page, press ___+__.

3 When you save a new web page, it's important that you name it with the appropriate file extension, such as _____ or _____.

4 The following statement defines a page margin.

    A The space between the content on a page and the monitor edge.

    B The space between the content on a page and the edges of the browser window.

    C The space between the content on a page and individual elements.

5 The hexadecimal code #3ba is short for _____.

6 How do you sort files in the Files panel?

7 When you double-click a file in the Files panel, the following statement is true.

    A The Open dialog box opens.

    B The Save As dialog box opens.

    C The file opens in the Document Window.

    D A warning box is displayed.

8 True or False: If you move a file into or out of a folder using the Files panel, Dreamweaver updates all relevant links automatically.

Unit 3

Basic editing

Complete this unit, and you'll know how to:

A Insert and import text from external files.

B Insert special characters.

C Use headings, paragraphs, and other structural elements to organize a web page into a logical hierarchy.

D Insert line breaks.

E Create unordered, ordered, and definition lists.

Topic A: Inserting and importing text

Explanation

You can add text to a web page by typing in the Document window. If the text is in a separate file, you can import the text or copy and paste it into Dreamweaver.

It's often helpful to use an external file as the source of your website text so you can distribute the file for editing and approval by other members of a development team. When the text is approved and ready, you can copy and paste it into Dreamweaver. You can import text from a text file or from a formatted document, such as a Microsoft Word document.

Importing text

You can import content by dragging a file from the Files panel to the open web page in the Document window. If you have a program that can open the file on your computer, such as Microsoft Word, then the Insert Document dialog box prompts you to specify your import and formatting preferences, as shown in Exhibit 3-1. If you don't have a program that can open the file, Dreamweaver will insert a link to the file.

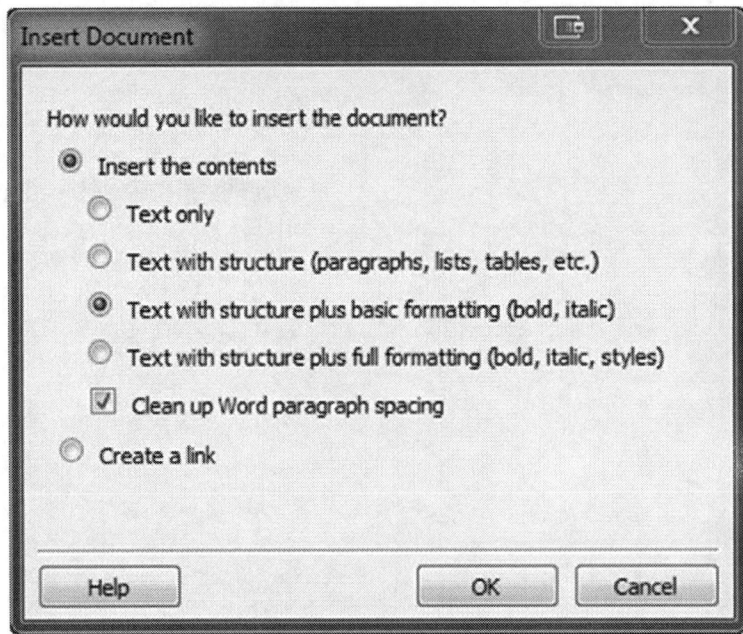

Exhibit 3-1: The Insert Document dialog box

The options in the Insert Document dialog box are described in the following table.

Option	Description
Insert the contents	Copies the file's text into the web page.
Text only	Inserts plain text without any formatting.
Text with structure	Inserts plain text and retains structures such as paragraph breaks, lists, and tables.
Text with structure plus basic formatting	Inserts plain or structured text. If any text uses basic formatting, such as boldface or italics, Dreamweaver retains this formatting by adding HTML tags when necessary.
Text with structure plus full formatting	Inserts plain or structured text and retains all HTML tags and internal CSS styles.
Clean up Word paragraph spacing	Removes extra spacing above and below paragraphs in documents imported from Microsoft Word.
Create a link	Inserts a hyperlink to the text file (rather than inserting the text itself).

Pasting text from other sources

Using the standard Copy and Paste commands is another way to bring content from another application into Dreamweaver. To control how Dreamweaver formats content pasted from another application, choose Edit, Paste Special. The formatting options in the Paste Special dialog box, shown in Exhibit 3-2, are the same as those in the Insert Document dialog box.

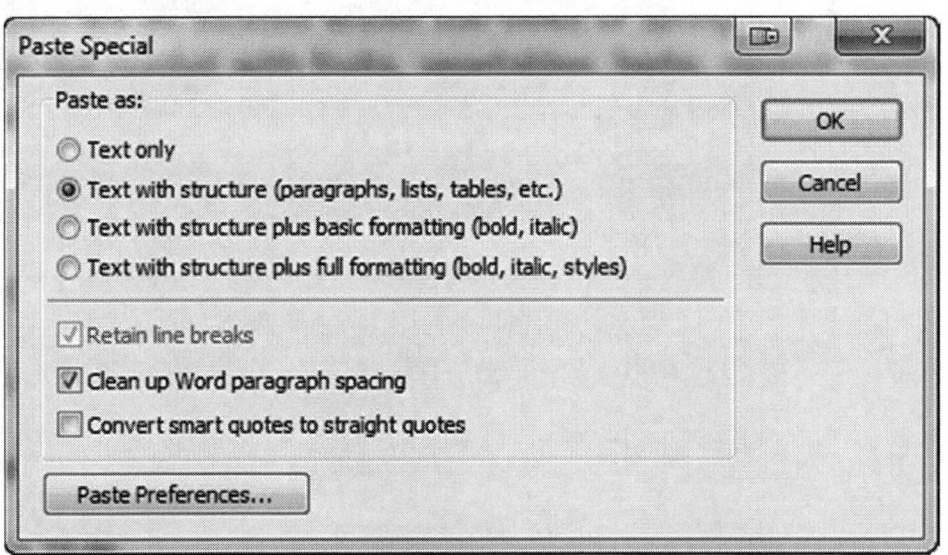

Exhibit 3-2: The Paste Special dialog box

Do it!

A-1: Importing text

The files for this activity are in Student Data folder **Unit 3\Topic A**.

Here's how	Here's why
1 Open the Site Setup for Harvest-Valley-Market dialog box	
Update the Local Site Folder location to the current unit and current topic	
2 Open the **Home** page	Double-click index.html in the File panel.
Switch to Design view	If necessary.
3 Select all of the text after the Welcome heading	

Welcome to Harvest Valley Market

Be aware that the CSS for these layouts is heavily commented. If you do most of your work in Design view, have a peek at the code to get tips on working with the CSS for the fixed layouts. You can remove these comments before you launch your site. To learn more about the techniques used in these CSS Layouts, read this article at Adobe's Developer Center - http://www.adobe.com/go/adc_css_layouts.

Layout

Since this is a one-column layout, the .content is not floated.

Logo Replacement

An image placeholder was used in this layout in the .header where you'll likely want to place a logo. It is recommended that you remove the placeholder and replace it with your own linked logo.

Be aware that if you use the Property Inspector to navigate to your logo image using the SRC field (instead of removing and replacing the placeholder), you should remove the inline background and display properties. These inline styles are only used to make the logo placeholder show up in browsers for demonstration purposes.

To remove the inline styles, make sure your CSS Styles panel is set to Current. Select the image, and in the Properties pane of the CSS Styles panel, right click and delete the display and background properties. (Of course, you can always go directly into the code and delete the inline styles from the image or placeholder there.)

	From "Be aware…" to "…from the image or placeholder there.)
Press `DELETE`	To delete all of the placeholder text.

4 Drag **HVM-Home1.doc** from the Files panel to the Document window below the Welcome heading	The Insert Document dialog box appears as shown in Exhibit 3-1. You'll import text from this Microsoft Word file and then from a simple text file.
5 Verify that **Insert the contents** is selected	
Verify that **Text with structure plus basic formatting (bold, italic)** is selected	To import the text and any basic formatting.
Verify that **Clean up Word paragraph spacing** is checked	To remove unnecessary spaces and returns and other unwanted characters from the Word document.
Click **OK**	To insert the text as specified. Notice that "Rain or shine" appears in bold and italics—the basic formatting was retained.
6 If necessary, place the insertion point as shown	located within 100 miles of Springfield. et with fruits, vegetables, herbs, organic crafts made by local artisans.│
Press ⏎ ENTER	To start a new paragraph.
7 Drag **HVM-Home2.txt** below the current text	(From the Files panel.) To add more text from another type of file. The Insert Document dialog box appears.
Click **OK**	To insert the text and close the Insert Document dialog box. This is a plain text file with no formatting.
8 Save and close the page	

Topic B: Using special characters

This topic covers the following Adobe ACE exam objectives for Dreamweaver CS6.

#	Objective
5.1	**Inserting special characters**
5.1.1	Describing situations that require inserting special characters
5.1.2	Understanding HTML encoding used for special characters

Special characters

Explanation

Some characters that you might need in your content are not included on a computer keyboard, such as the copyright symbol (©) or language-specific characters like the umlaut (ü). You can insert these special characters in Code view by entering their corresponding *character entities*, which are HTML codes that begin with an ampersand (&) and end with a semicolon. The following table lists some common examples.

Character	Symbol	HTML code
Copyright	©	&copy;
Registered trademark	®	&reg;
Degree	°	&deg;

Inserting special characters

The codes required for these special characters aren't always intuitive or easy to remember, so Dreamweaver provides a list of hints. To insert a special character:

1 In Code view, place the insertion point where you want the special character to appear.

2 Type & (ampersand). A list of hints for special characters appears.

3 Scroll through the list to find the desired character. The HTML code for the character appears in the right column in black, and the character appears in the left column in blue.

4 Select a character from the list.

Extra spaces

When you're working in Design view, you can't insert more than one standard space between words. To insert more than one space, you need to switch to Code view and use the *non-breaking space* character ( ). This special character adds a single space without forcing a line break.

Do it! **B-1: Inserting special characters and spaces**

The files for this activity are in Student Data folder **Unit 3\Topic B**.

Here's how	Here's why
1 Open the Site Setup for Harvest-Valley-Market dialog box	
Update the Local Site Folder location to the current unit and topic	
2 Open the Home page	(From the Files panel.) You'll create a copyright symbol in the page footer.
3 Switch to Code view	
Scroll to the bottom of the page	You'll replace the word "Copyright" with the copyright symbol.
Double-click **Copyright**	`<div class="footer">` `    <p>`Copyright`</p>`
	To select it. (You can also drag to select it.)

4 Type **&**	`<div class="footer">`
	`    <p>&</p>`
	`<!-- ` "
	`<!-- ` & &
	` &lt;`

	A list appears, showing a variety of special characters.

Type **co**	`<div class="footer">`
	`    <p>&co</p>`
	`<!-- ` © ©
	`<!-- end` © ≅

	The copyright symbol is selected in the list. (You could also scroll through the list to locate the character you're looking for.)
Press ⏎ ENTER	To insert the copyright symbol.
5 Switch to Design view	
6 After the symbol type as shown	© Harvest Valley Market. All Rights Reserved.
	To finish the standard copyright declaration.
7 Scroll up to view **This Week's Specials** text	Notice there needs to be spaces added after the colons for each special.

8 Switch to Code view

9 In Code view, place the insertion
   point before **Aged** as shown

```
<p>This Week's Specials</p>
<p>Artisan Breads and Cheeses:Aged Sharp
```

You'll insert a space after the colon.

Press (SPACEBAR) two times   To insert two spaces in the HTML code.

10 Switch to Design view

Observe the two spaces   Even though you entered two spaces, only one
space displays on the page.

11 Switch to Code view and delete   (Press Backspace two times.) You'll insert non-
the two spaces   breaking spaces instead.

12 Type **&**   To display the list of special characters.

Type **nb**   To select nbsp; from the list.

Press (↵ ENTER)   To insert a non-breaking space.

13 Insert one more non-breaking
space, as shown

```
<p>This Week's Specials</p>
<p>Artisan Breads and Cheeses:  Aged Sharp
```

14 Switch to Design view   The two non-breaking spaces create additional
space between the colon and text.

15 Save and close the page

Topic C: Adding structure

This topic covers the following Adobe ACE exam objectives for Dreamweaver CS6.

#	Objective
5.4	**Understanding paragraph and header tags**
5.4.1	Benefits of using the appropriate tags to contain text content
5.4.2	Setting text format (P, H1, etc.) in the Property inspector

Document structure

Explanation

Headings, paragraphs, and other structural elements allow you to organize a web page into a logical hierarchy, which can make your pages more searchable, easier to read and easier for other developers to modify. A well-designed page structure can also make it easier to design and arrange your page content and make your content accessible to users with alternative browsing devices.

There are many ways to build a web page, but it's important that you use HTML tags in their proper context to define a meaningful page structure. For example, if you want to create a heading for a page or a section, you should define the text as a heading and not simply change the appearance of the text to *resemble* a heading.

Headings

When you're creating a document that requires multiple headings and subheadings, think of it as a traditional outline. The heading level you choose should logically reflect the nature of the content. HTML includes six headings that you can use to structure your documents—Heading 1 through Heading 6. The tags for these headings are `<h1>` through `<h6>`.

Browsers apply their own default formatting to these headings, which you can change using a style sheet. Headings are bold by default, and they use different font sizes. The `<h1>` tag applies the largest default font size, and the `<h6>` tag applies the smallest default font size.

So, for a heading that serves as the top-level heading on a page, you should define it as Heading 1. To do so, select the text, and in the Property inspector, select Heading 1 from the Format list. In the code, the text will be defined by the `<h1>` tag. You can also manually enclose the text in an `<h1>` tag if you prefer to work in Code view.

Paragraphs

To define a block of text as a paragraph, click inside the text block and select Paragraph from the Format list in the Property inspector. If you need to divide a block of text into separate paragraphs, simply place the insertion point where you want to begin a new paragraph and press Enter.

Creating meaningful and logical document structures establishes consistency on your pages, saves you time and effort when you later update your pages, and allows your pages to be indexed by search engines more efficiently. Focusing on establishing a meaningful document structure typically results in an efficient document with a small file size, or page weight, especially when all style-related information is contained in an external style sheet. The smaller the file size, the faster the page will load.

For example, if you're creating a page intended to deliver company news, an effective structure might look something like this:

```
<h1>Company News</h1>
<p>First paragraph of Company News...</p>
<p>Second paragraph of Company News...</p>
<h2>Subheading of Company News</h2>
<p>First paragraph of subtopic...</p>
```

Block quotes

If you have a line or block of text that's a quotation, you can define it as such to distinguish it from other text. First click inside the text (or select the text) and then click the Blockquote button in the Property inspector. A `<blockquote>` tag is inserted to define the text. By default, block quotes are indented on both sides.

Do it!

C-1: Defining headings and paragraphs

The files for this activity are in Student Data folder **Unit 3\Topic C**.

Here's how	Here's why
1 Open the Site Setup for Harvest-Valley-Market dialog box	
Update the Local Site Folder location to the current unit and topic	
2 Open **visiting-the-market.html**	From the Files panel.
Switch to Split view	Working in Split view makes it easier to see the changes in both the design and the code.
3 Place the insertion point in the **Visiting Harvest Valley Market** text	(At the top of the page.) Click once in the line of text.
In the Property inspector, observe the Format for the text	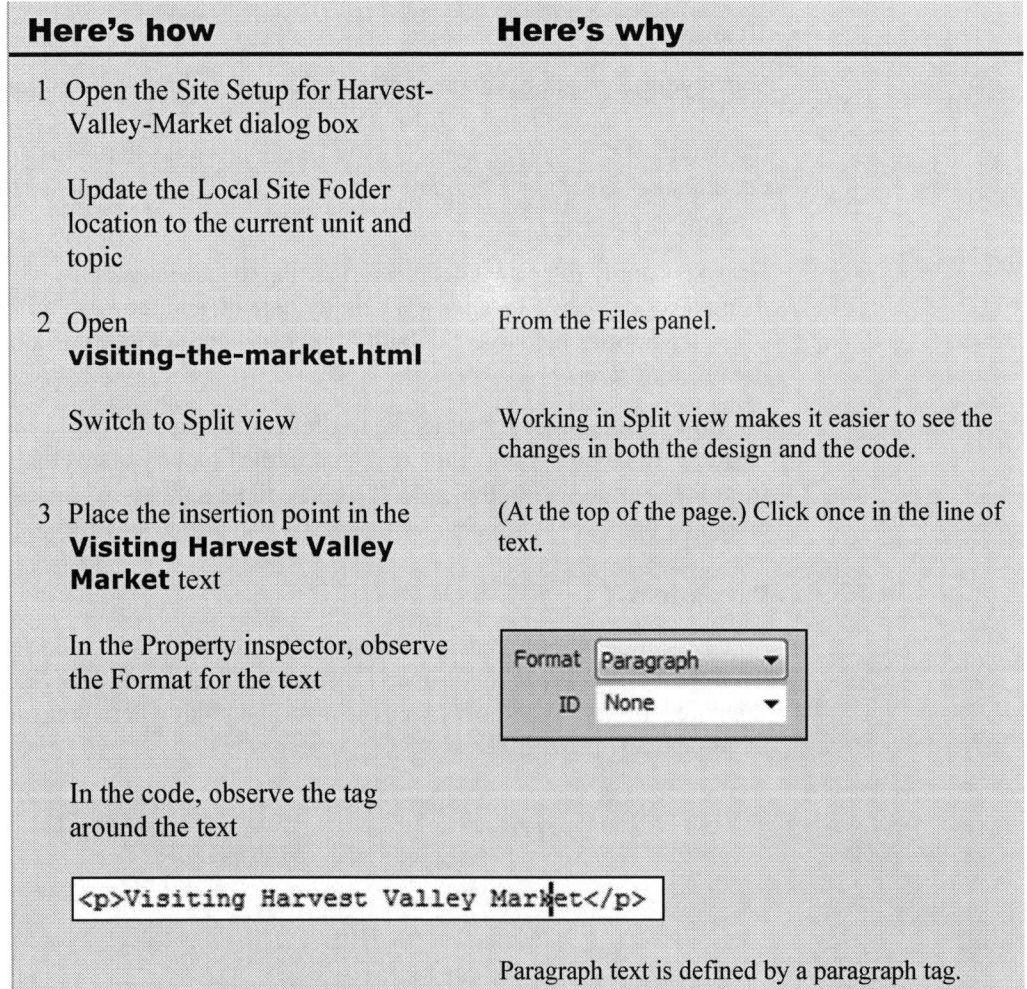
In the code, observe the tag around the text	

```
<p>Visiting Harvest Valley Market</p>
```

Paragraph text is defined by a paragraph tag.

4	In the Property inspector, from the Format list, select **Heading 1**	To convert the text to a level-one heading. Browsers render level-one headings a certain way by default, but you can change the formatting with a style sheet.
5	In the code, observe the heading code	The text is now enclosed in <h1> tags to define it as a top-level heading.
6	Place the insertion point in the **Weather** text	Scroll down, if necessary.
	Covert the text to a level-two heading	(Select Heading 2 from the Format list in the Property inspector.) This heading is not quite as large as Heading 1.
7	Convert the **Parking**, **Shopping Tips**, **Pets**, and **Getting Help** text to level-two headings	
8	Observe the block of text under each of the headings	The text blocks are not defined by any HTML tags. You'll define them as paragraphs.
9	Click anywhere inside the text block under **Visiting Harvest Valley Market**	To place the insertion point.
	Observe the format in the Property inspector and the code	In the Property inspector, the Format list reads "None" because this text is not defined by any HTML element. In the code, there are no tags around the text.
10	From the Format list, select **Paragraph**	The text block is now defined as a paragraph.
	Observe the format in the Property inspector and in the Code view	Note that the text is now contained in a <p> tag. It's important that you always put your text content inside a paragraph tag or another HTML tag, depending on the purpose of the content.
11	Define the remaining text blocks as paragraphs	
12	Place the insertion point in the **Rain or Shine!** paragraph	At the top of the page. You'll create a block quote.
	Click 🔳	(The Blockquote button is in the Property inspector.) To define the text as a block quote.
13	Switch to Design view and observe the formatting changes	
	Save and close the page	

Topic D: Inserting line breaks

This topic covers the following Adobe ACE exam objectives for Dreamweaver CS6.

#	Objective
5.5	**Inserting line breaks**
5.5.1	Understanding the difference between <p> and tags

Line breaks and paragraphs

Explanation

When you're adding text in a web page, the web browser will display the text as a long line until it reaches the edge of the browser window or container element. Then the text will wrap to the next line. When you are entering text in the Document Window and you press Enter, Dreamweaver by default, starts a new paragraph and inserts an open and closing paragraph tag with a non-breaking space character ( ) between the two tags. Once you enter some text, the non-breaking space character is replaced with your text.

But sometimes you might not want a new paragraph that has white space between the lines of text. In this case, you want to enter a line break. The syntax for a line break is a single tag, <br />. To enter a line break in Design view, place your cursor at the end of the line, then hold Shift and press Enter.

Do it!   **D-1:   Inserting line breaks**

The files for this activity are in Student Data folder **Unit 3\Topic D**.

Here's how	Here's why
1 Open the Site Setup for Harvest-Valley-Market dialog box Update the Local Site Folder location to the current unit and topic	
2 Open **visiting-the-market.html**	
3 Switch to Split view	To see both the Code and Design panes.
4 In the Weather paragraph, click as shown	to the weather. The market is an outdoor ost to blazing heat. Don't get dehydrated! t their booths.
	(In the Design view) To place the insertion point.
Press (⏎ ENTER)	To create a new paragraph.
In the code, observe the new paragraph	You created a separate paragraph simply by pressing the Enter key.
5 Click as shown	avoid the crowds. The busiest times
	(In the Design view, under Shopping Tips) To place the insertion point.
Press (SHIFT) + (⏎ ENTER)	To move the text down one line.
In the code, verify there is now a ` ` tag	In Design view, pressing Shift+Enter does not create a new paragraph but instead inserts a line break, the ` ` tag. (The `<p>` tag was already there.) Line breaks force text down one line within the paragraph.
6 Switch to Design view and observe the changes Save and close the page	

Topic E: Creating lists

This topic covers the following Adobe ACE exam objectives for Dreamweaver CS6.

#	Objective
5.6	**Creating lists**
5.6.1	Understanding 3 types of lists: bullet, numbered, definition
5.6.2	Indenting list items in the Property inspector

Lists

Explanation

You can create unordered, ordered, and definition lists. (Unordered lists are also called *bulleted lists*, and ordered lists are also called *numbered lists*.) In an unordered list, a bullet (black circle), square, or custom icon precedes each list item. By default, an unordered list uses black bullets, as shown in Exhibit 3-3. Use an unordered list when the sequence of the list items is not important or relevant. The HTML tag `<ul>` starts an unordered list, and each list item is defined by an `<li>` tag.

Shopping Tips

- Bring sturdy shopping bags or baskets.
- Bring small bills and change.
- Come early for the best selection.
- Come after 10:00 am to avoid the crowds.

Exhibit 3-3: An unordered list

In an ordered list, a number or letter indicates each item's order in the list, as shown in Exhibit 3-4. By default, ordered lists are numbered 1, 2, 3, and so on. You can also choose Alphabet Large (A, B, C), Alphabet Small (a, b, c), Roman Large (I, II, III), or Roman Small (i, ii, iii). Use an ordered list when the sequence of items is important.

The `<ol>` tag starts an ordered list, and each list item is defined by an `<li>` tag.

Vendor Booths

1. Artisan Breads and Cheeses
2. Cattle Ridge Ranch
3. Fairview Gardens
4. Good Organics
5. Johnson Family Farm

Exhibit 3-4: An ordered list

Definition lists

You can also create a definition list, which doesn't use bullets or numbers. A definition list is used for terms and their definitions and is often used in glossaries, "frequently asked questions" pages (FAQs), and similar contexts. As shown in Exhibit 3-5, each definition is indented beneath its term. This indentation is the only default formatting that browsers apply to a definition list. You might consider making the definition terms bold to distinguish them from the definition text.

```
Artisan Breads and Cheeses
    We are located at booth 1. We offer fresh, homemade cheese, artisan breads, and fresh herbs.
Cattle Ridge Ranch
    Come and visit us at booth 2. We have grain fed beef and pork and a variety of homemade sausages.
```

Exhibit 3-5: A definition list

The `<dl>` tag starts a definition list, as shown in Exhibit 3-6. Each term is wrapped in a `<dt>` tag and definition text is wrapped in a `<dd>` tag, which stands for definition description.

```
<dl>
<dt>Artisan Breads and Cheeses</dt>
    <dd>We are located at booth 1. We offer fresh, homemade cheese, artisan breads,
        and fresh herbs.</dd>
<dt>Cattle Ridge Ranch</dt>
    <dd>Come and visit us at booth 2. We have grain fed beef and pork and a variety
        of homemade sausages.</dd>
</dl>
```

Exhibit 3-6: Code for a definition list

Creating a list

To create a list, you can select paragraphs of text and convert them to list items by clicking the Unordered List button or the Ordered List button in the Property inspector. You can also choose Format, List and then choose Unordered List, Ordered List, or Definition List. Each selection starts a new list. You can then begin typing, and when you press the Enter key, a new numbered or bulleted list item will appear. To complete the list, press Enter twice.

After you create a list, you can change the list type or style if necessary. Click any list item and then click List Item in the Property inspector. This opens the List Properties dialog box. Select the desired list type and style, and then click OK.

Nested lists

A *nested list*, also called a *sub-list,* is a list inside another list. For example, a step in a list of instructions might require its own list of sub-steps. To make a sub-list, select the content that you want to turn into a nested list and click the Indent button in the Property inspector. Indenting a list item also changes its default bullet style, which helps to establish the hierarchical structure of the list.

Do it!

E-1: Creating lists

The files for this activity are in Student Data folder **Unit 3\Topic E**.

Here's how	Here's why
1 Open the Site Setup for Harvest-Valley-Market dialog box Update the Local Site Folder location to the current unit and topic	
2 Open **visiting-the-market.html**	(Double-click the file in the Files panel.) You'll convert ordinary text to an unordered list.
3 Switch to Design view	If necessary.
4 Select all paragraphs under the **Shopping Tips** heading, as shown	

Shopping Tips

Bring sturdy shopping bags or baskets.
Bring small bills and change.
Come early for the best selection.
Come after 10:00 am to avoid the crowds.
The busiest times at the market are between 9:00 am and 11:00 am.
Don't be afraid to ask questions.
How is it grown?
How do you cook it?
Who has a certain kind of product?
Our vendors love getting to know their customers and are happy to share

You'll convert these paragraphs to a single unordered list.

5 In the Property inspector, click 📋	(The Unordered List button.) To format the selected text as an unordered list.
6 Click anywhere on the page	

Shopping Tips

- Bring sturdy shopping bags or baskets.
- Bring small bills and change.
- Come early for the best selection.
- Come after 10:00 am to avoid the crowds.
  The busiest times at the market are between 9:00
- Don't be afraid to ask questions.
- How is it grown?
- How do you cook it?
- Who has a certain kind of product?
- Our vendors love getting to know their customers a

To deselect the text. The paragraphs were converted to items in an unordered list, which is a more appropriate structure for this content.

7 Switch to Code view

Observe the code for the unordered list

Each item in the list is defined by the `<li>` tag, and all the list items are nested inside the `<ul>` tag, the unordered list tag.

```
31        <h2>Shopping Tips</h2>
32        <ul>
33          <li>Bring sturdy shopping bags or baskets.</li>
34          <li>Bring small bills and change.</li>
35          <li>Come early for the best selection. </li>
```

Switch to Design view

8 Select the three questions under **Don't be afraid to ask questions.**, as shown

- Don't be afraid to ask questions.
- How is it grown?
- How do you cook it?
- Who has a certain kind of product?

You'll indent these list items to create a nested list.

9 In the Property inspector, click ⬚

(The Text Indent button.) To indent this part of the list, creating a sub-list or "nested" list. The items are indented and have a different default bullet style. You can change the bullet type for a list by using CSS.

10 Choose **Format**, **List**, **Properties...**

To open the List Properties dialog box.

From the Style list, select **Square**

To change the bullets for the nested list to squares.

Click **OK** and deselect the text

- Don't be afraid to ask questions.
  - How is it grown?
  - How do you cook it?
  - Who has a certain kind of product?

To apply the new bullet style to the selected items.

11 Save and close visiting-the-market.html

12 Open vendor-booths.html

13 Select the paragraphs under **Vendor Booths**, as shown

Vendor Booths

Artisan Breads and Chees
Cattle Ridge Ranch
Fairview Gardens
Good Organics
Johnson Family Farm
Nuts & Berries
Old Friends Ranch
Ozark Farm
Smith's Organic Ranch
Summer Hills Farm
Two Lanes Farms
Winding Creek Ranch

You'll convert these paragraphs into an ordered list.

14 In the Property inspector, click [icon]

(The Ordered List button.) To convert the text to an ordered list.

Deselect the text

Vendor Booths

1. Artisan Breads and Cheeses
2. Cattle Ridge Ranch
3. Fairview Gardens
4. Good Organics
5. Johnson Family Farm
6. Nuts & Berries
7. Old Friends Ranch
8. Ozark Farm
9. Smith's Organic Ranch
10. Summer Hills Farm
11. Two Lanes Farms
12. Winding Creek Ranch

(Click anywhere on the page.) To view the results. The text is now an ordered list.

15 Switch to Code view

Observe the code for the ordered list

Each item in the list is defined by the `<li>` tag, and all the list items are nested inside the `<ol>` tag, the ordered list tag.

Switch to Design view

16 Save and close vendor-booths.html

17	Create a new, blank HTML page	Choose File, New; verify that Blank Page, HTML, and <none> are selected; and click Create.
18	Choose **Format**, **List**, **Ordered List**	To create an ordered list. The number 1 is displayed on the page.
	Type **Spring Produce** and press ⏎ ENTER	The number 2 is displayed as the next list item.
	Type **Summer Produce** and press ⏎ ENTER	To create a third list item.
	Type **Fall Produce** and press ⏎ ENTER two times	To end the list.
19	Click any of the list items	To place the insertion point.
	In the Property inspector, click **List Item...**	To open the List Properties dialog box.
	From the Style list, select **Alphabet Small (a,b,c...)**	
	Click **OK**	To format the ordered list in alphabetical order using lowercase letters.
20	Close the file without saving it	

Unit summary: Basic editing

Topic A   In this topic, you learned how to **import text** from other sources. You also learned how to copy and paste text from other sources to a web page.

Topic B   In this topic, you learned about situations that require inserting **special characters**. You learned the HTML encoding used for special characters and how to insert these characters into the HTML code.

Topic C   In this topic, you learned how to apply **structural tags**, including headings and paragraphs. You also learned that an efficient and meaningful page structure can make it easier to maintain a Web site, as well as to design and arrange page content.

Topic D   In this topic, you learned the difference between a **paragraph break** and a **line break**. You also learned how to insert each type of break in the code.

Topic E   In this topic, you learned how to create unordered, ordered, and definition lists. You also learned how to indent lists to create nested **lists**.

Independent practice activity

In this activity, you'll convert text to headings, import text files, and create unordered lists.

The files for this activity are in Student Data folder **Unit 3\Unit summary**.

1 In the Site Setup for Practice-Harvest-Valley-Market dialog box, update the Local Site Folder location to the current unit summary folder.

2 Open local-produce.html.

3 Convert the **Local Produce** text to a level-one heading.

4 Convert the **Spring Seasonal Produce**, **Summer Seasonal Produce**, and **Fall Seasonal Produce** text to a level-two heading.

5 Add a blank line under the Spring Seasonal Produce heading, and import the **Spring Produce.txt** file.

6 Add a blank line under the Summer Seasonal Produce heading, and import the **Summer Produce.txt** file.

7 Add a blank line under the Fall Seasonal Produce heading, and import the **Fall Produce.txt** file.

8 Convert the lists under each level-two heading to an unordered list and change the bullet style for each list to square.

9 Remove the blank lines at the end of each list, if necessary.

10 Save and close local-produce.html.

Review questions

1 True or False: You can import content by dragging a file from the Files panel to the open web page in the Document window.

2 The character entity for the registered trademark symbol (®) is _____.

3 To insert more than one space, switch to Code view and use the non-breaking space character which is _____.

A

B &space;

C :

D &space:

4 How many heading levels does HTML provide for the purpose of structuring documents?

5 To add a line break in Design view, hold _____ and press _____.

6 The following is the syntax for a line break.

A `<br><br />`

B `<brk><brk />`

C `<br />`

D `<brk />`

7 A bulleted list is called a(n) _____ list.

8 A numbered list is called a(n) _____ list.

9 A nested list is also called a(n) _____ list.

Unit 4
CSS basics

Complete this unit, and you'll know how to:

A Explore CSS basics.

B Create external style sheets.

C Define and apply element styles to text as well as use class styles.

D Explore the cascade effect.

Topic A: Overview of style sheets

This topic covers the following Adobe ACE exam objectives for Dreamweaver CS6.

#	Objective
6.1	**Understanding basic CSS syntax**
6.1.1	Describing 4 main selectors (Class, ID, Tag, and Compound)
6.1.2	Describing 3 locations for CSS (inline, HTML head, external)
6.1.4	Understanding that CSS rules specify properties of elements
6.1.5	Understanding that CSS can format and position page items
6.3	**Applying styles using the Property inspector**
6.3.4	Setting the ID of a selected element in the HTML section

Introduction to CSS

Explanation

By itself, HTML provides limited design capability. Browsers apply default styles to many elements, such as headings, paragraphs, block quotes, and tables, but these default styles are typically not enough to achieve the design you have in mind. *Cascading Style Sheets (CSS)* is the standard style language for the Web. CSS and HTML work together; HTML provides the basic structure, and CSS controls how the elements within that structure appear in a browser.

Control, efficiency, and consistency

Using CSS, you can fully control the design and layout of your pages. For example, you can control the fonts, margins, spacing, colors, and borders that produce your site's look and feel. You can also control the layout of the page's elements, such as where the navigation is located or if the page has multiple columns for content.

What makes CSS especially powerful is that you can link multiple pages to a style sheet, and therefore update all of your pages by changing the style rules in one file. Style sheets mean zero redundancy; all of your site's style-related information is stored in a single location instead of being repeated on each page. This leads to faster, simpler design updates and cleaner, more efficient pages that load quickly and consistently.

Internal and external style sheets

You can define and apply styles for HTML elements by using external style sheets, internal style sheets, and inline styles.

- **External style sheet** — A collection of style rules that are defined in a text file, saved with a .css extension, and linked to your web pages. Use external style sheets whenever you want the styles to be global—that is, when you want them to apply to multiple pages in a site. When you change a style in an external style sheet, the change is reflected in every page linked to that style sheet.

- **Internal style sheet** — A collection of style rules defined in the <head> section of an HTML document. Internal styles (also called *embedded styles*) apply only to the page in which they're defined. Use an internal style sheet when you need a style for only a single page or when you want to override a style in an external style sheet.

- **Inline styles** — Another type of CSS style; they apply formatting directly to a single instance of an element. To create an inline style, you use the `style` attribute of any rendered HTML tag in conjunction with CSS properties. However, inline styles are a discouraged method because the style information is not kept separate from the HTML code, which eliminates one of the key benefits of using style sheets—the ability to update styles from a central location while keeping the HTML free of unnecessary clutter.

Do it!

A-1: Discussing style sheets

The files for this activity are in Student Data folder **Unit 4\Topic A**.

Questions and answers
1 What's a style sheet?
2 What are the two main types of style sheets?
3 What are the advantages of using an external style sheet?
4 When might you want to use an internal style sheet?
5 How can using external style sheets help reduce the size of your HTML files?

Selector types and their syntax

CSS rules specify properties of elements and have the following syntax:

```
selector { property: value; }
```

The *selector* defines what page element the style applies to. The *declaration* is either empty or consists of a property name, followed by a colon (:), followed by a property value. Multiple declarations for the same selector may be organized into semicolon (;) separated groups. Exhibit 4-1 shows an example of a CSS rule with the selector and declaration defined.

Tag selector

```
body {
    font: 100%/1.4 Verdana, Arial, Helvetica, sans-serif;
    background-color: #CCCCCC;
    margin: 0;
    padding: 0;
    color: #000;
}
```

— Declaration

Exhibit 4-1: Tag selector and declaration

There are many types of selectors you can use. The most commonly used selector types are described in the following table.

Selector	Description

Tag selectors	Also called element selectors or element styles, these style rules define the formatting of individual HTML tags. An element style overrides the default formatting for that HTML element. The syntax to define an element style is:
	
	`tag { property: value; }`
	
	For example, if you want paragraphs to appear bold, write:
	
	`p { font-weight: bold; }`

Class selectors	Class selectors allow you to give elements names that are meaningful to you. For example, you can create a class of the \<p\> element named "important" that applies bold, red text. Any paragraphs that are given that class name will appear with those styles. You can apply class styles to multiple elements on a page. The syntax for a class style is:
	
	`.className { property: value; }`
	
	Class names begin with a period. For example, to manually create the rule mentioned above, you'd write:
	
	`.important { font-weight: bold; color: red; }`
	
	A semicolon separates each style property. A style rule can contain any number of properties.

Selector	Description

ID selectors	ID selectors also allow you to create and name your own elements. However, while a class style can be applied to multiple elements in a page, an ID style can be applied only once per document. ID styles are particularly useful for defining major content sections. The syntax for an ID style is:
	
	`#IDname { property: value; }`
	
	IDs begin with the pound sign (#). For example:
	
	`#footer { font-size: 10px; color: gray; }`

Compound selectors	Compound selectors can be used to combine two or more style rules to create a style definition that displays only when one style is contained within another. Compound styles are useful when you want to use the same tag multiple times on the same web page but with different formatting. Compound styles are created by combining ID, class, or tag styles and the syntax is: `#IDname tag { property: value; }` In a compound style, you must include a space between each name or tag, but don't include the brackets around a tag in a style name.

More advanced selector types include pseudo-class selectors and contextual or "descendent" selectors. Pseudo-class selectors are used to style hyperlinks in their various user-defined states, while descendent selectors target elements that exist in a particular context. For example, you can apply styles to only those paragraphs that are inside a Div tag with the ID name "content".

Do it!

A-2: Discussing selector types and their syntax

The files for this activity are in Student Data folder **Unit 4\Topic A**.

Questions and answers

1   Name three selector types that you can define in a style sheet.

2   If you want the text of *all* level-one headings in your site to be blue, what type of selector should you use?

3   Describe a scenario in which you'd want to use a class selector.

4   Describe a scenario in which you'd want to use an ID selector.

Topic B: External style sheets

This topic covers the following Adobe ACE exam objectives for Dreamweaver CS6.

#	Objective
6.1	**Creating and managing CSS styles in the CSS Styles panel**
6.1.2	Describing 3 locations for CSS (inline, HTML head, external)
6.1.4	Understanding that CSS rules specify properties of elements
6.1.5	Understanding that CSS can format and position page items
6.1.7	Setting color properties with hexadecimal values
6.2	**Creating and managing CSS styles in the CSS Styles panel**
6.2.1	Linking an external CSS style sheet to a web page
6.2.2	Creating a new CSS style in the panel

Creating external style sheets

Explanation

To create a new, blank external style sheet:

1 Choose File, New to open the New Document dialog box.
2 Select Blank Page (if necessary).
3 From the Page Type list, select CSS.
4 Click Create.
5 Save the file and name it with a .css extension. (Save it in a folder dedicated to style sheets, inside your site folder.)

Creating CSS rules manually

When you create a style sheet, it opens in Code view. You can begin entering CSS rules manually, or you can create them by using the CSS Styles panel. To create a rule manually, type it on a new line. For example, to create a rule that gives all level-one headings a font size of 24 pixels, you would type:

```
h1 {font-size: 24px;}
```

As mentioned earlier, the element to the left of the braces is the *selector*—the element that will be styled. The styles (one or more properties and their values) must be inside the braces. In this example, the property is `font-size`, which is followed by a colon. After this comes the property's value, in this case, `24px`.

The semicolon is used to separate one style from the next. If a rule has only one style declaration, you don't need a semicolon, but it's a good idea to place one there anyway, in case you decide to add more properties to the rule.

Using the CSS Styles panel

You can modify CSS styles directly in a style sheet, or you can use the CSS Styles panel to view, create, edit, and delete rules and attach the style sheet to your Web site's pages. To open the CSS Styles panel, choose Window, CSS Styles.

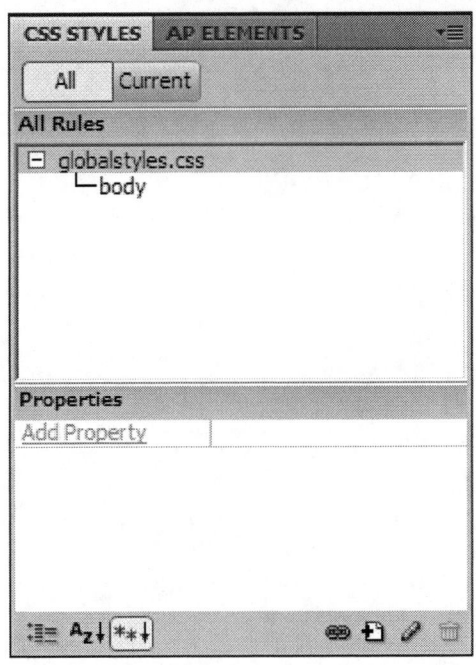

Exhibit 4-2: The CSS Styles panel, showing one style rule in globalstyles.css

Link an external style sheet to a web page

To link a Web page to an external style sheet:

1. Open the Web page.
2. At the bottom of the CSS Styles panel, click the Attach Style Sheet button (the chain-link icon). The Attach External Style Sheet dialog box opens.
3. Click Browse to open the Select Style Sheet File dialog box.
4. Navigate to and select the .css file you want to use.
5. Click OK to close the Select Style Sheet File dialog box.
6. Click OK to attach the file and close the Attach External Style Sheet dialog box.

Do it!

B-1: Creating an external style sheet

The files for this activity are in Student Data folder **Unit 4\Topic B**.

Here's how	Here's why
1 Open the Site Setup for Harvest-Valley-Market dialog box	
Update the Local Site Folder location to the current unit and topic	
2 Open index.html	Observe the formatting and layout that is applied to the page. A good portion of the formatting and layout is defined by an external CSS sheet.
3 Observe the CSS Styles panel	If necessary, choose Window, CSS Styles.
Click the **Switch to All** button	
	If necessary.
Expand **globalstyles.css**	If necessary.
Observe the CSS rules	(Scroll down.) These CSS rules are applied to web pages linked to this sheet.
4 Verify **globalstyles.css** is selected	In the CSS Styles panel.
Click the **Unlink CSS Stylesheet** button	
	To remove the external style sheet.
5 Observe index.html	(In Design view.) The text is displayed with the default styles applied. Also, notice that the location of the photograph has changed. Next, you'll create your own style sheet.
6 Choose **File, New...**	To open the New Document dialog box.
Verify that **Blank Page** is selected	You'll create a new, blank style sheet.
From the Page Type list, select **CSS**	
Click **Create**	An untitled style sheet file opens in Code view.

7 Click in line 4

```
1  @charset "utf-8";
2  /* CSS Document */
3
4  |
```

Type **body {**   A list of CSS properties appears.

Type **backg**

```
body {backg
          background
          background-attachment
          background-clip
          background-color
          background-image
          background-origin
          background-position
          background-repeat
          background-size
```

As you type, the list updates.

In the list, double-click   A list of value options appears.
background-color

Double-click **Color...**   A color palette appears and the pointer changes
                                     to an eyedropper.

8 Click the pale yellow color shown

```
          #FFC
```

To give the `<body>` element (the visible part of
the Web page) a pale yellow background color.

Type **;}**   To close the style rule.

9 Choose **File**, **Save**   To open the Save As dialog box.

Double-click the **css** folder   To open it. You'll save the style sheet in this
                                     folder.

Observe globalstyles.css   The link was deleted in the CSS Styles panel but
                                     the file itself wasn't deleted.

In the File name box, type | File name: | HVMstyles.css |
HVMstyles.css

Click **Save**   (Or press Enter.) To save the style sheet.

10	In the CSS Styles panel, view all styles	(If necessary.) Click the Switch to All (Document) Mode button.
	Expand the style sheet and observe	The rule you created for the `<body>` element appears.
11	View index.html	(In Design view.) You'll attach the style sheet to this page.
	Observe the CSS Styles panel	The style sheet does not appear because this page is not linked to it.
12	Click 🖳	(The Attach Style Sheet button is at the bottom of the CSS Styles panel.) The Attach External Style Sheet dialog box appears.
	Click **Browse**	To open the Select Style Sheet File dialog box.
	Open the css folder	
13	Select **HVMstyles.css**	
	Click **OK**	To attach the style sheet to this page and close the Select Style Sheet File dialog box.
	Verify that **Link** is selected	To create a link to this style sheet.
	Click **OK**	To close the Attach External Style Sheet dialog box. The page now has a pale yellow background because the color is applied to the `<body>` element in the style sheet. You'll edit this style in the CSS Styles panel.
14	Switch to Code view	
	Locate the link to the style sheet	(In line 6.) The code now includes a link to globalstyles.css.
	Switch to Design view	
15	In the CSS Styles panel, click **body**	(If necessary, expand HVMstyles.css.) To select the rule.
	Click **#FFC**	Properties for "body" background-color ▾ #FFC Add Property To edit this color value.
	Type **#fff** and press ⏎ ENTER	To change the background color to white. This is one way you can quickly edit style rules.

16	Open history.html	From the Files panel.
	In the CSS Styles panel, click [icon]	To open the Attach External Style Sheet dialog box, which is automatically populated with the most recent path and file name.
	Click **OK**	To attach the page to the style sheet.
17	Unlink the globalstyles style sheet	(In the CSS Styles panel, select globalstyles and click the Unlink CSS Stylesheet button.) To view the style sheet you just created.
18	Observe the Related Files toolbar	(Under the Document tab.) HVMstyles.css is displayed because it's now attached to the page. You can click the style sheet name to open the file.
19	Save and close history.html	(If prompted, save HVMstyles.css.) In the next activity, you'll continue to modify the index.html page and the style sheet.
	Close HVMstyles.css and index.html	If prompted, save the files.

Topic C: Creating styles

This topic covers the following Adobe ACE exam objectives for Dreamweaver CS6.

#	Objective
1.3	**Updating properties in the Property inspector**
1.3.2	Understanding HTML vs. CSS sections of Property inspector
6.1	**Understanding basic CSS syntax**
6.1.8	Using common CSS measurement values (%, pixel, and em)
6.2	**Creating and managing CSS styles in the CSS Styles panel**
6.2.3	Editing a CSS style in the CSS Rule Definition dialog box
6.2.4	Adding and deleting rules in the Properties pane
6.3	**Applying styles using the Property inspector**
6.3.1	Applying a style using the Target Rule list in the CSS section
6.3.2	Using the Edit Style option in the CSS section
6.3.3	Setting the Class of a selected element in the HTML section

Creating and applying element styles

You can define the appearance of an HTML element by using the HTML tag name as the selector in the style rule. When you define an element style in a global style sheet, every instance of that element across the site will pick up the style. This feature helps to ensure a consistent appearance and makes style updates fast and easy.

To use the CSS Styles panel to create an element style:

1 Open the web page or style sheet.

2 In the CSS Styles panel, click the New CSS Rule button.

3 From the Selector Type list, select Tag (defines an HTML element).

4 From the Selector Name list, select the HTML tag (element) to which you want to apply the style.

5 Under Rule Definition, do one of the following:

- Select a style sheet. This option will add the rule to the style sheet. (This option will not be displayed if the active document is a style sheet.)

- Select (New Style Sheet File). This option will add the rule to a new style sheet.

- Select (This document only). This option will embed the rule in the active document. If you select this option with a web page active, the style will be applied to that page only.

6 Click OK.

7 In the CSS Rule Definition dialog box, set the desired attributes for the style.

8 Click OK.

Editing styles in the CSS Rule Definition dialog box

After creating a style, you can edit it. Start by selecting the style rule in the CSS Styles panel, and then click the Edit Rule button to display the CSS Rule Definition dialog box. Modify the style attributes and click OK.

Creating and editing styles in the Property inspector

The Property inspector provides another way to quickly apply new styles to your pages. Click the CSS button, shown in Exhibit 4-3, to display the CSS options. Then, either select a rule from the Targeted Rule list, or create a rule. Click the Edit Rule button to open the CSS Rule Definition dialog box for the selected rule. You can also quickly apply some of the most common styles, including font, font size, color, and text alignment.

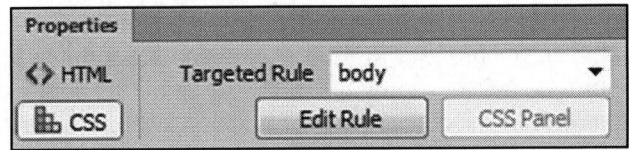

Exhibit 4-3: CSS rule controls in the Property inspector

To switch between styles or to remove a style, display the Targeted Rule list and select another option.

Typography basics

Explanation

There are many typographical styles that you can apply to text, including the font (typeface), font size, and weight (degree of boldness).

Font-size units

To control font size, there are several units of measurement you can use, including points and pixels. Points are a unit of print measurement that does not translate well to the screen. Pixels are a more appropriate choice for the Web. Using pixels typically produces the most consistent results across various browsers and platforms.

Font sets

A *font set* is a list of similar fonts. When you apply a font set, the user's web browser tries to display text in the first font specified in the set. If the first font isn't available on the user's computer, the browser looks for the second font in the set. If that font isn't available, the browser tries to apply the third font in the set, and so on. A font set should end with a generic font—serif, sans serif, or monospaced. This practice guarantees that even if a user doesn't have any of the fonts listed in your font set, at least the general font type will be applied.

Serif and sans serif fonts

The difference between serif and sans serif fonts is the style in which the letters are formed. A serif font has *flourishes* (decorations) at the ends of its characters, while sans serif fonts don't, as illustrated in Exhibit 4-4. In monospaced fonts, such as Courier and Courier New, each character takes up the same amount of horizontal space. Monospaced fonts resemble typewriter text.

Exhibit 4-4: Serif and sans serif fonts

Do it!   ### C-1: Defining element styles

The files for this activity are in Student Data folder **Unit 4\Topic C**.

Here's how	Here's why
1 Open the Site Setup for Harvest-Valley-Market dialog box	
Update the Local Site Folder location to the current unit and topic	
2 Open index.html	
3 In the Property inspector, click ⊞ CSS	To display the CSS options.
In the Targeted Rule box, verify that **body** is selected	Targeted Rule body
	You'll apply styles to the <body> element, and these styles will be inherited by all other elements in the document.
4 From the Font list, select the font of your choice	(The font listed will depend on what fonts are installed on your computer.) The text on the page changes to the new font because every element inherits the styles of the <body> element, the topmost parent element.
From the Size list, select **12**	Size 12 ▼ px ▼
	To set the size of the body text to 12 pixels. The text on the page is smaller, except for the headings.
5 Why don't the headings inherit the font size of the body rule?	
6 In the CSS Styles panel, click ⊕	(The New CSS Rule button.) The New CSS Rule dialog box opens. You'll create a style rule for all level-one headings.
Under Selector Type, select **Tag**	You'll define an element style, meaning that it applies to all instances of a specific HTML tag.
From the Selector Name list, select **h1**	To apply this rule to the <h1> element.
Under Rule Definition, verify that **HVMstyles.css** is selected	This rule will apply to all level-one headings on pages attached to this style sheet.
Click **OK**	The CSS Rule Definition dialog box opens.

7 In the Font-size box, type **20** — To give all level-one headings a font size of 20 pixels.

8 Click the Color box — To open the color palette.

Select a dark green color

Click **OK** — To apply the new style. The level-one heading text is now green and smaller than its default size.

9 Scroll down the page to view the This Week's Specials heading — This heading did not pick up the style because it's a level-two heading, defined by the <h2> element.

10 Open the New CSS Rule dialog box — In the CSS Styles panel, click the Create New CSS Rule button.

From the Selector Type list, select **Tag**

From the Selector Name list, select **h2** and click **OK** — To create a style rule for level-two headings.

11 From the Font-size list, select **16**

Apply an orange text color — Click the Color box and select an orange color from the palette.

Click **OK** — To apply the new element style.

12 Observe the CSS Styles panel — The h1 and h2 rules appear in the style tree, and the properties of the selected rule are displayed.

13 On the Related Files toolbar, click **HVMstyles.css**

To view the changes in the style sheet.

Observe the new CSS code — You can modify the CSS code directly in the style sheet, or you can use the Property inspector and the CSS Styles panel to create and edit styles.

Choose **File**, **Save** — To save your changes in the style sheet.

14 Click **Source Code** — (On the Related Files toolbar.) To display the code for the index.html page.

Switch to Design view

15 Save index.html

Class styles

Explanation

Class styles allow you to share styles among different HTML elements and to name your elements, thus giving added meaning to your document structure. For example, let's say you want to apply a style to just one paragraph among several. You can't achieve this by changing the style definition for the <p> tag, because that will affect *all* paragraphs. Instead, you can create a class style and apply it to only the paragraph where it's needed.

Class names

Give your class styles meaningful names to make maintenance easier, both for you and for others who might work on the site in the future. For example, a year from now, it'll be easier to determine how a class style was meant to be used if it's named "discount" instead of "class2."

Creating class styles

As with all CSS styles, you can create class styles in internal or external style sheets. To create a class style:

1 Open the web page or style sheet.

2 In the CSS Styles panel, click the New CSS Rule button.

3 In the New CSS Rule dialog box, under Selector Type, select Class.

4 In the Name box, type a meaningful name. (Class styles must begin with a period, and Dreamweaver automatically adds the period before the class name.)

5 Under Rule Definition, do one of the following:

- Select a style sheet. This option will add the class to the style sheet. (This option will not be displayed if the active document is a style sheet.)

- Select (New Style Sheet File). This option will add the class to a new style sheet.

- Select (This document only). This option will embed the class in the active document. If you select this option with a web page active, the style will be applied to that page only.

6 Click OK.

7 In the CSS Rule Definition dialog box, define the attributes for the style.

8 Click OK.

C-2: Creating class styles

The files for this activity are in Student Data folder **Unit 4\Topic C**.

Here's how	Here's why
1 Observe the text at the top of the page	Open Year Round Tuesday through Saturday, 6 am to 1 pm Local Produce | Fresh Herbs | Baked Goods | Organic Meats
	Under the graphic.
Place the insertion point in the Open Year Round text	
On the Properties panel, click the **HTML** button	To activate the HTML options.
Observe the Format list	This line of text is a Heading 3.
2 What format is applied to the second and third line of text?	
3 Open the New CSS Rule dialog box	In the CSS Styles panel, click the New CSS Rule button.
4 Under Selector Type, select **Class**	
In the Name box, type **topnavbar**	Dreamweaver automatically adds the period before the class name.
Under Rule Definition, verify **HVMstyles.css** is selected	
Click **OK**	To create the class style and open the CSS Rule Definition for .headerright in HVMstyles.css dialog box. Next, you'll define the class style attributes.
5 Under Category, verify Type is selected	
From the Font-family list, select the font of your choice	(To define the font attribute.) Choose the same font you selected in the previous activity.
In the Color text box, type **#030**	To change the font color attribute to dark green.
6 Under Category, select Block	To display text spacing and alignment attributes.
From the Text-align list, select **center**	
7 Click **OK**	To close the dialog box.

Applying class styles

After you create a class style, you need to apply it to one or more elements. The class styles you create appear in the Targeted Rule list in the Property inspector. To apply a class style, select an element on the page and then select the class style from the Targeted Rule list.

Setting the Class of a selected element in the HTML section

You can also apply a class style using the HTML section of the Property inspector. To do so, select an element on the page and click the HTML button on the Property inspector. From the Class list, select the class name.

C-3: Applying class styles

The files for this activity are in Student Data folder **Unit 4\Topic C**.

Here's how	Here's why
1 Select the three lines of text at the top of the page	Drag to select "Open Year Round" to "Organic Meats." Make sure to select all the text.
2 On the Properties panel, click the **CSS** button	To activate the CSS options.
3 From the Targeted Rule list, select **topnavbar**	You can also use the CSS Styles panel to apply the class style.
4 Deselect and observe the text	(In Design view). The H3 and H4 headings have the same font, font color and alignment applied to them.
5 Display HVMstyles.css in Code view	
Observe lines 17-21	Those lines contain the .topnavbar class style. It is applied to all three lines of text regardless of what HTML tag is applied to them.
6 In Design view, select **Open Your Round**	
In the Properties panel, display the Targeted Rule list and select **<Remove Class>**	To remove the .topnavbar class from the Heading 3 text.
7 Observe the text	The first H3 no longer has the .topnavbar class applied. The second line, which is also an H3, does have the class applied, and so does the last line (an H4 heading).
8 Save HVMstyles.css	
Save and close index.html	

Topic D: Cascade effect

This topic covers the following Adobe ACE exam objectives for Dreamweaver CS6.

#	Objective
6.1	**Understanding basic CSS syntax**
6.1.3	Understanding the cascade effect (which rules are applied)

The cascade

Explanation

The style applied to an element can be specified in many different places, which can interact in a complex way. This complex interaction makes CSS powerful, but it can also make it confusing to learn, as well as provide opportunity for styles conflicts.

To understanding how CSS works, you need to be clear about how the three main sources of style information form a *cascade*. The style sources are:

- Default styles specified by the browser for the markup language.
- Styles specified by a user who is reading the web page.
- Styles specified by the web page author using external style sheets, internal styles, and inline styles.

The user's styles modify the browser's styles. The web page author's style then modifies the style some more, resulting in potential style conflicts. The "cascading" part of Cascading Style Sheets refers to the way CSS resolves such style conflicts. The general rule is this: The closer the style rule is to the element that is being styled, the more weight the rule is given. Also, the more specific the rule, the more weight it's given.

Inheritance

This concept of specificity also relates to inheritance. *Inheritance* is the process by which properties are passed from parent to child elements even though those properties have not been explicitly defined by other means. For example, if you apply font styles to the <body> element, every element on the page will inherit those styles because the <body> element is the parent element of every rendered element on the page. Similarly, if you have a <div> tag that contains three paragraphs (<p> tags), and you apply font and color styles to the <div> tag, those three paragraphs will inherit the styles.

As you apply styles to your pages, you can use inheritance to your advantage. Inheritance helps eliminate redundancy and complexity, resulting in smaller and more efficient style sheets that are easy to update.

There are some exceptions to the general rule of style inheritance. Not every CSS property can be inherited, and some elements, like headings, have their own default font sizes.

Importance

Sometimes you find that the cascade or inheritance is resulting in an undesired style on your web page. To overcome this, you can increase the importance of your declarations by adding the !important statement to the end of the declaration using the following syntax:

```
.navbar { property: value !important; }
```

Declarations are sorted in the following order (from lowest to highest priority):

- Browser declarations
- Normal declarations in user style sheets
- Normal declarations in author style sheets
- Important declarations in author style sheets
- Important declarations in user style sheets

Do it!

D-1:   Examining the cascade effect

The files for this activity are in Student Data folder **Unit 4\Topic D**.

Here's how	Here's why
1 In the Manage Sites dialog box, click **New Site**	
Name the site as **Cascade-Effect-Example**	
For the site location, browse to the **Cascade Effect Example** folder	Located in the current unit and topic folder.
Click **Save** and **Done**	To define the local folder.
2 Open cascade-example.html	
3 Observe the Example Text	It is a level-one heading with a green color applied to it.
Observe the text under the heading	It explains that the <H1> element has three conflicting CSS rules applied to it.

4 In Split view, place the insertion point in line 17

Observe the style color applied to the `<h1>` tag

#030 is the green color applied to the sample text. This is the inline style has the highest priority and so it is applied in the cascade effect.

```
16   <p>This example demonstrates the cascade effec
17   <h1 style="color:#030">Example[ Text</h1>
18   <p>This Heading 1 has three conflicting style
```

In the Property Inspector, display the CSS options and observe the Color text box

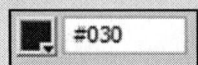

This also shows the inline style color that is applied to the text.

5 In the CSS Styles panel, click the All button

If necessary.

Expand **`<style>`** and select **h1**

CSS Styles | AP Elements

All | Current

All Rules

⊟ ExampleStyleSheet.css
  └ h1
⊟ <style>
  └ h1

This is the internal style sheet that contains properties applied to the <h1> tag.

Observe the properties

According to this style, the H1 heading should be blue (#00F), but due to the style conflict, it is not applied.

6 In the CSS Styles panel, expand **ExampleStyleSheet.css** and select **h1**

This in the external style sheet that contains properties applied to the <h1> tag.

Observe the properties

This defines the H1 heading as red (#F00) but is not applied due to the cascade effect.

7	In the code pane of Split view, select as shown	(In line 17.) Select the space after "<h1" to "#030."

```
16      <p>This example demonstrates the cascade effect
17 ⊟ <h1 style="color:#030">Example Text</h1>
18      <p>This Heading 1 has three conflicting style ru
```

	Press (DELETE)	The remaining tag should be <h1>.
	In the Properties panel, click ↻ Refresh	To update the code.
8	Observe the heading text	(Deslect the text, if necessary.) Since the internal style sheet is next in the list of priorities, the blue color (#00F) is applied.
9	Open ExampleStyleSheet.css	
	Place the insertion point after #F00	(And before the semi-colon in the code pane of Split view.)
10	Press (↵ ENTER)	
	Type **!i** and double-click **!important**	
	In the CSS Styles panel, click **Refresh**	To update the code.
11	Observe the heading text	The !important declaration overrides the normal cascade order and the H1 text is now red (#F00).
12	Save and close cascade-example.html	If prompted, save changes to ExampleStyleSheet.css as well.

Unit summary: CSS basics

Topic A In this topic, you explored the basics of **internal** and **external style sheets**, as well as the syntax of CSS rules.

Topic B In this topic, you learned how to **create an external style sheet**, use the CSS Styles panel, and the CSS options on the Property inspector.

Topic C In this topic, you learned how to define and apply **element styles** and **class styles**.

Topic D In this topic, you explored the basics of the **cacade effect**, inheritance, and learned how to use the !important statement.

Review questions

1 The following is a collection of CSS style rules that are defined in a text file, saved with a .css extension, and linked to your web pages.

   A External style sheet

   B Internal style sheet

   C Inline styles

2 The following is a collection of CSS style rules defined in the <head> section of an HTML document.

   A Inline styles

   B External style sheet

   C Internal style sheet

3 The following applies CSS formatting directly to a single instance of an element.

   A Internal style sheet

   B Inline styles

   C External style sheet

4 If you want all of the level-two headings in your site to share the same formatting, you should:

   A Create an internal element style for the <h2> tag.

   B Create an external element style for the <h2> tag.

   C Create an internal class style.

   D Create an external class style.

5 If you want to create a special type of paragraph with extra large text, and you think you'll need to use the style for multiple paragraphs on a page, it's best to:

   A Create an internal element style for the <p> tag.

   B Create an external element style for the <p> tag.

   C Create an external class style and give it a meaningful name.

   D Create an external ID style and give it a meaningful name.

6 If you want to define a unique section that holds the navigation bar and you want this element to look the same on every page, it's best to:

  A Create an internal class style and give it a meaningful name, such as navbar.

  B Create an external class style and give it a meaningful name, such as navbar.

  C Create an internal ID style and give it a meaningful name, such as navbar.

  D Create an external ID style and give it a meaningful name, such as navbar.

7 True or false? A class named "introduction" is likely to be more meaningful and effective than a class named "style3."

8 True or false? When you create a style for the `<h1>` element for a page that contains that element, all you need to do is define the style and it's applied automatically.

9 True or false? When you create a class style, the style is automatically applied on the page.

Independent practice activity

In this activity, you'll edit the external style sheet and add an internal style sheet that includes both an element style and a class style.

The files for this activity are in Student Data folder **Unit 4\Unit summary**.

1 In the Site Setup for Practice-Harvest-Valley-Market dialog box, update the Local Site Folder location to the current unit summary folder.

2 Using the CSS Styles panel, edit the external style sheet named **globalstyles.css** to make all level-one headings **purple** and **30px**.

3 Open all seven HMTL pages to verify the headings have been updated.

4 On index.html, add an internal style sheet that makes the level-one heading **blue** and **36px**. (*Hint:* On the CSS Styles panel, click the New CSS Rule button. In the Selector Type list, select Tag. In the Selector Name list, select the desired tag name. In the Rule Definition list, select (This document only).)

5 Compare the heading on index.html to the other web pages.

6 View index.html in Design view. Add a class style to the internal style sheet named **rainshine**. In the CSS Rule definitions for .rainshine dialog box, change the type options to include **italic** and font color **#333**.

7 Select the paragraph that begins **Rain or shine, our vendors…** and apply the **.rainshine** class style. (*Hint:* In the Property inspector, use the Targeted Rule list.)

8 Save and close all open files.

Unit 5

Images, multimedia, and links

Complete this unit, and you'll know how to:

A Add graphics to a web page by inserting images, placeholders, and rollovers as well as defining image attributes.

B Edit images in Dreamweaver and in an external image editor.

C Add multimedia to a web page by inserting Flash SWF and FLV files.

D Discuss hyperlink basics.

E Connect web pages by creating internal and external links, using named anchors, and applying link styles.

Topic A: Working with images

This topic covers the following Adobe ACE exam objectives for Dreamweaver CS6.

#	Objective
8.1	**Inserting images**
8.1.1	Requirement of saving image files in the local root folder
8.1.2	Inserting placeholder images while designing a site
8.1.3	Inserting rollover images
8.1.4	Benefits of adding Alternate text for SEO and accessibility
8.1.6	Understanding images should be at original size (don't scale)

Images on the Web

Explanation

Images are an integral part of web design. They catch the user's eye, they can introduce a unique artistic aspect to site designs, and they can often deliver information in a way that text can't. For example, images of products give potential buyers visual information that can't be matched by a text description.

File size is a vital consideration when you use images on web pages. Large image files can take a long time to load in a user's browser. Try to keep your image file sizes as small as possible without sacrificing quality.

File formats

The three main image formats supported by web browsers are GIF, JPEG, and PNG. GIF images, which can contain a maximum of 256 colors, are best used for images with relatively few colors and with areas of flat color, such as line drawings, logos, and illustrations. GIFs also support animation and transparency. The GIF format isn't recommended for photographs or illustrations with complex color gradations. When you save simple images with fewer than 256 colors, GIF uses a *lossless* compression algorithm, which means that no image data is discarded to compress the image.

The JPEG format supports more than 16 million colors, so it's best for photographs and images that have many subtle color shadings. JPEG uses *lossy* compression, which means that some image data is discarded when the file is saved.

The PNG format combines some of the best features of JPEG and GIF. It supports more than 16 million colors, so it's ideal for photos and complex drawings. It can use a variety of lossless compression algorithms, and it supports many levels of transparency, allowing areas of an image to appear transparent or semitransparent.

The following table summarizes these three image file formats.

	GIF	JPEG	PNG
Best used for:	Simple images with few colors	Photographs	Photographs or simple images
Maximum colors	256	More than 16 million	More than 16 million
Compression	Lossless	Lossy	Lossless
Transparency	One level (complete transparency)	Not supported	Multiple levels

Images folder

Dreamweaver stores all the files associated with your website on your hard drive in a folder defined as your *local site folder*, which is also called your websites' *root folder*. When you insert an image onto a web page, the file must be contained within your local site folder so that all references to it are correct.

Within the root folder, web designers will often use subfolders with relevant names to manage the different file types. A sample folder structure is shown in Exhibit 5-1.

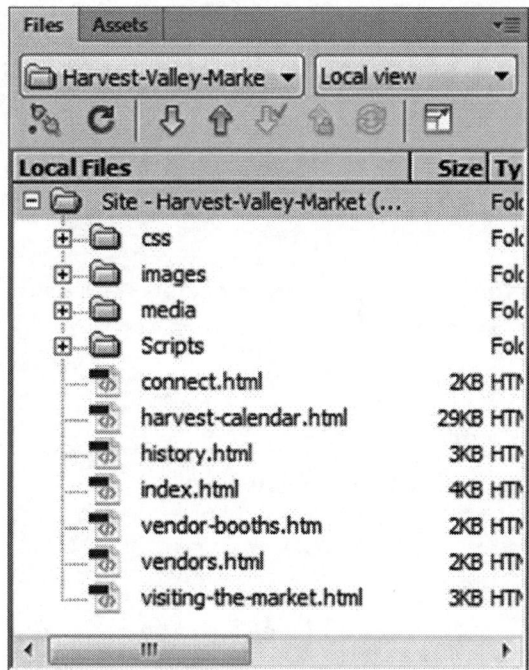

Exhibit 5-1: Sample folder structure

You can create and manage your website's folder structure in the Files panel. In the case of the images folder, you can also define its default location in the Site Setup dialog box. Here's how:

1 Open the Site Setup dialog box for the current website.
2 In the left pane, expand Advanced Settings and select Local Info.
3 In the right pane, click the Browse for folder button, which is located to the right of the Default Images folder text box.
4 Navigate to the desired folder and click Select.
5 Click Save and Done.

Do it!

A-1: Discussing image formats

Questions and answers

1 Which image formats are typically best for photographs?

2 Which image formats support transparency?

3 True or false: The GIF format and the JPEG format support the same number of colors.

4 A corporate logo that contains text and six colors is probably best saved in which image format?

5 Why is it important to limit the file size of your images?

Adding images

Explanation

You can use images to convey or reinforce ideas in ways that text alone cannot. A web page that includes images is often more visually appealing and inviting to the user than is a page with just text.

To insert an image in a web page:

1 If necessary, create a subfolder in the site folder and place all the image files in it. Give the folder a logical name, such as "images."
2 In the Files panel, navigate to the folder containing the images for the current site.
3 Drag an image file to the Document window.
4 In the Image Tag Accessibility Attributes dialog box, type a meaningful text alternative and click OK.

You can then adjust the size and position of an image by using the options in the Property inspector. In the Property inspector, you can also add or modify alternate text by using the Alt box.

Accessibility and alternate text

When you add an image, Dreamweaver prompts you to provide alternate text for it. Doing this is important for ensuring accessibility. Accessible web design entails using simple methods that help make your content operable on a variety of devices, beyond the standard visual browsers like Internet Explorer, Safari, Firefox, and Chrome.

For example, users with visual impairments are likely to use alternative browsing devices such as screen readers and Braille printers. These devices can access any text content, but they can't read or describe an image, so they rely on the text alternative that you specify. Alternate text should describe either the content or the purpose of the image, whichever is most appropriate.

It's important to make an effort to ensure that your site content is accessible to these devices. Doing so can also help to establish a loyal user base.

Use proper punctuation in your Alt text

If your Alt text is a complete sentence or is made up of multiple sentences, you should always use proper punctuation. Screen readers use punctuation to emulate the natural pauses and inflections in speech.

Search Engine Optimization (SEO)

Another reason to use Alt text is for Search Engine Optimization (SEO) marketing purposes. Most search engines use Alt text values to determine what is contained within objects like photographs. So, it is good idea to add Alt text for all your images that include relevant key words your readers might use when performing a web search.

Do it!

A-2: Inserting images

The files for this activity are in Student Data folder **Unit 5\Topic A**.

Here's how	Here's why
1 Open the Site Setup for Harvest-Valley-Market dialog box	
Update the Local Site Folder location to the current unit and topic	
2 In the Files panel, expand the images folder	Resize the Files panel within the Panels Group, if necessary.
Observe the files	All the images associated with this website are contained within this folder.
3 Open history.html	
4 Select the image in the top-left corner	It is named harvest-valley-market-png150px.png.
5 Observe the Property inspector	The Src text box points to the file in the images folder. The Alt txt box contains the alternate text value. The W and H boxes list the width and height pixel values. The Class list contains the CSS style name.
6 Drag **peaches.jpg** to the Document window	From the images folder in Files panel.
Point to the left of **Our History** heading	Without release the mouse button
Release the mouse button	To place the image in this location. The Image Tag Accessibility Attributes dialog box opens.
7 In the Alternative text box, type **Peaches**	
Click OK	
8 Observe the image	
Observe the Property inspector	You can change the Src file path, the Alt text, and CSS Class among other options.
9 Save the file	

Image attributes

Explanation

When you drag an image onto a page, Dreamweaver writes the HTML code required to embed the image. This code consists of the image tag (`<img>`) and several attributes, which are properties for the element. The location of the `<img>` tag tells the browser where to embed the file, and the `src` attribute tells the browser where to find the image file.

You can set image attributes by using the Property inspector. The attributes of the `<img>` tag are described in the following table.

Attribute	Use	Description
src	Required	Specifies the path to the image file.
alt	Recommended	Provides alternate text. If the browser can't display the image, alternate text provides access to the text in the image or a description of the image, whichever is more appropriate.
height	Recommended	Specifies the height of the image. Although you can change the size of an image by setting a different height or width, it is better to resize your image outside of Dreamweaver for the best display.
width	Recommended	Specifies the width of the image.

If you are familiar with previous versions of Dreamweaver and are looking for the vspace, hspace, align or border attributes, they are no longer available in the Property inspector. Those attributes are considered deprecated in HTML. Instead, you can use the corresponding CSS declarations to produce the same results.

Do it!

A-3: Setting image attributes

The files for this activity are in Student Data folder **Unit 5\Topic A**.

Here's how	Here's why
1 Select the peaches image	If necessary.
2 In the Property inspector, click the **Toggle Size Constrain** icon	 To unlock the proportional constraint applied to the image.
3 Change the W box to **250** Press ⏎ ENTER	 To change the width of the image. Notice that the image appear distorted because it wasn't changed proportionally.
Change the H value to **250** and press ⏎ ENTER	The image is no longer distorted. Since the image was originally created to be viewed at 150 x 150 pixels, the image clarity is gone. When you want to change the size of an image, a better solution is to resize the image in an application like Adobe Fireworks using the original file, export the image, and then insert the exported file in Dreamweaver.
4 Press CTRL + Z twice	To undo the changes.
5 Click the **Browse for File** button	 To open the Select File dialog box.
Navigate to the images folder	If necessary.
Double-click **squash.jpg**	To close the dialog box and replace the image.
6 In the Alt box, select **Peaches** Type **Squash**	 To replace the alternate text value.
7 Save the file	

Placeholder images

Explanation

Let's say that you and a colleague are designing a website. You are responsible for the layout and your partner is supplying all the images. Instead of waiting until you have the final artwork, you can work on the layout by using placeholder images to define the size and location of the images. Here's how:

1 Place the insertion point in the Document window.

2 Choose Insert, Image, Image Placeholder.

3 In the Image Placeholder dialog box, set the following options:

- In the **Name** box, enter an optional label for the image placeholder.
- In the **Width** and **Height** boxes, enter the required image size in pixels.
- Set the optional **Color** value.
- In the **Alternate text** box, enter the optional word or phrase that describes the final image.

4 .Click OK to insert an image placeholder as shown in Exhibit 5-2.

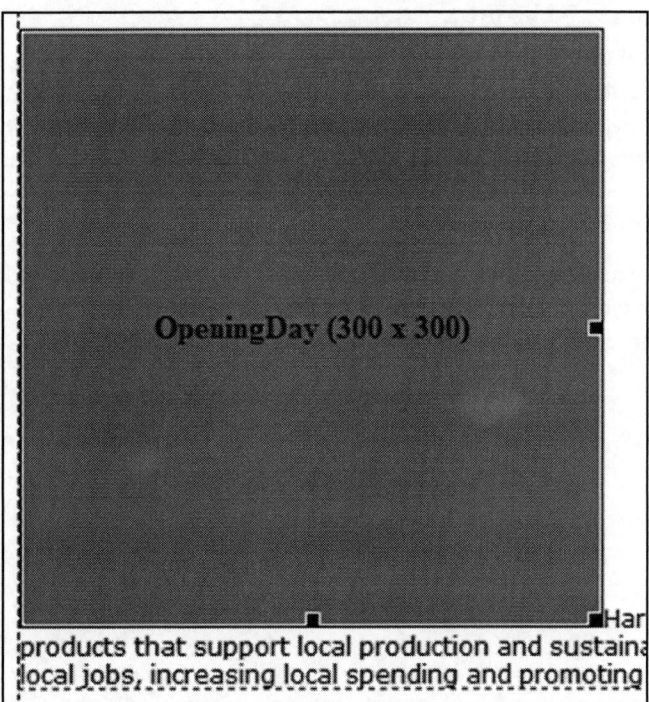

Exhibit 5-2: Placeholder image

Once the image placeholder has been created, you can select it and make adjustments to it by using the Property inspector.

Alternative methods for creating an image placeholder images

The following steps provide an alternative method for creating the example shown in Exhibit 5-2:

1 Insert an image without Alt text.

2 Select the image on the page.

3 In the Property inspector:

- In the ID box, enter "OpeningDay"

- In the Src box, delete the file path.

- Verify the Alt box is empty.

- In the W and H boxes, change the values to "300."

If you prefer, you can also create an image placeholder by editing the HTML code. Here's how to create the example shown in Exhibit 5-2:

1 Insert an image.

2 Switch to Code view or Split view, and locate the `<img>` tag associated with the image you inserted.

3 Edit the code to remove the values in the scr and alt attributes, change the width and height values, and add a name attribute. Your tag now looks like:

```
<img src="" width="300" height="300" alt=""
name="OpeningDay" />
```

Replace an image placeholder

To replace an image placeholder with the final artwork, double-click the placeholder to open the Select Image Source dialog box. Navigate to the correct folder, select the image, and click OK.

Do it!   ### A-4:   Using placeholder images

The files for this activity are in Student Data folder **Unit 5\Topic A**.

Here's how	Here's why
1 Place the insertion point to the left of **Harvest Valley Market is**	At the beginning of the second paragraph under the Our History heading. You don't have the image yet, but you'll be adding a photograph that was taking during opening day in 1993.
2 Choose **Insert**, **Image**, **Image Placeholder**	(Or on the Insert bar in the Common tab, click the arrow to the right of the Images button and select Image Placeholder.) To open the Image Placeholder dialog box.
3 In the Name box, type **OpeningDay**	With no spaces.
In the Width box, type **300**	
In the Height box, type **300**	
Using the Color picker, select the color of your choice	
In the Alternative text box, type **From Opening Day in 1993**	
4 Click **OK**	To insert the placeholder as shown in Exhibit 5-2.

Rollover images

Explanation

A rollover image is an interactive web page element. In its most basic form, the primary image loads with the web page and is replaced with a secondary image when the mouse point hovers over it. Examples of rollover images include interactive buttons and tabs that change color when you point at them. To create a rollover:

1 Place the insertion point in the Document window.

2 On the Insert bar in the Common tab, click the arrow to the right of the Images button and select Rollover Image.

3 In the Insert Rollover Image dialog, set the desired options:

- Enter a unique name in the **Image Name** text box.

- To the right of the **Original image** text box, click Browse. Navigate to the desired folder and double-click the image that will load with the web page.

- To the right of the **Rollover Image** text box, click Browse. Navigate to the desired folder and double-click the image that will load when the user points their mouse at the original image.

- Check **Preload Rollover Image** to avoid any delay when the rollover is initiated.

- In the **Alternate Text** box, enter a description that for text-only browsers can use. This is optional.

- Use the **When clicked, Go to URL** text box or Browse button to identify the file, web page location, or website address that the browser opens when a user clicks the rollover image.

4 Click OK

5 Preview the page in a browser by pressing F12 or Shift+F12. When the page loads, point to the original image and it will be replaced with the rollover image.

When creating a rollover image, make sure the two images are the same size

Do it!

A-5:   Inserting rollover images

The files for this activity are in Student Data folder **Unit 5\Topic A**.

Here's how	Here's why
1 Select the squash image	On the Document window.
Press (DELETE)	You'll replace the image with a rollover image.
2 Verify the insertion point is to the left of **Our History**	
On the Insert bar in the Common tab, click the arrow to the right of the Images button	
Select **Rollover Image**	To open the Insert Rollover Image dialog box.
3 In the Image name box, enter **Onions**	
4 To the right of the Original image text box, click **Browse**	
Navigate to the images folder	If necessary.
Double-click **onions.jpg**	To select the file and return to the Insert Rollover Image dialog box.
5 To the right of the Rollover image text box, click **Browse**	
Double-click **onions-bw.jpg**	This image is the exact same size as the original image.
6 In the Alternative text box, enter **HVM onions are available year round.**	
7 Click OK	
8 Switch to Live View	(Click the Live button.) To preview the rollover.
Point to the rollover image	The onions.jpg is replaced with the onions-b&w.jpg image.
9 Click **Live**	To return to Design view.
Save and close the file	

Topic B: Editing images

This topic covers the following Adobe ACE exam objectives for Dreamweaver CS6.

#	Objective
8.2	**Using the Property inspector to update and edit images**
8.2.1	Understanding the crop, sharpen, brightness/contrast tools
8.2.2	Using round-trip editing to launch external image editors

Editing tools in the Property inspector

Explanation

Dreamweaver includes some basic image editing tools in the Property inspector, as shown in Exhibit 5-3, that do not require an image-editing application to be installed on your computer.

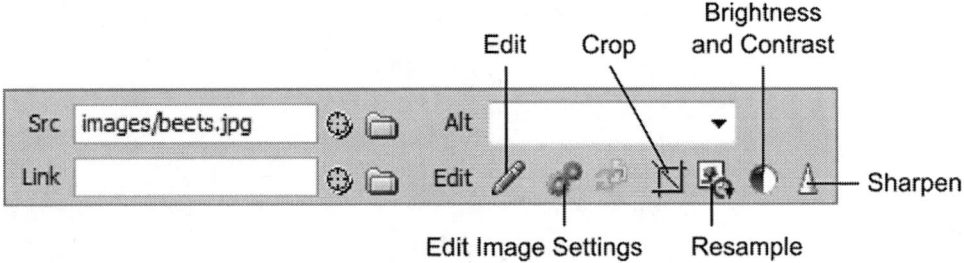

Exhibit 5-3: Editing tools available on the Property inspector

Resample

After resizing a bitmap image in Dreamweaver, click the Resample tool to add or subtract pixels in an attempt to match the original appearance of the image. While resampling an image does reduce file size, the results often also reduce image quality. The better solution is to resize the image in an external image editor application.

Crop

If you want to remove unwanted parts of an image, select an image and click the Crop button to display the crop handles around the image. Drag the handles until the part of the image you want to keep is surrounded. To complete the crop, double-click the image or press Enter.

Brightness and Contrast

If you think an image is too dark or too light, click the Brightness and Contrast button to open the Brightness/Contrast dialog box. Move the slides to adjust the image's highlights, shadows, and midtones. Click OK.

Sharpen

If an image appears too soft or out of focus, click the Sharpen button to open the Sharpen dialog box. Move the slide to increase the brightness along the edges of an image. Click OK.

Edit Image Settings

To optimize an image, verify the image is selected and click the Edit Image Settings button to open the Image Optimization dialog. From the Preset list, select one of the following options:

- PNG24 for Photos (Sharp Details)
- JPEG for Photos (Continuous Tones)
- PNG8 for Logos and Text
- JPEG High for Maximum Compatibility
- GIF for Background Images (Patterns)
- PNG32 for Background Images (Gradients)

Based on your selection in the Preset list, the Format list will be automatically populated and other options will be available at the bottom of the dialog box. Make the desired edits and click OK.

Do it!

B-1:   Editing images within Dreamweaver

The files for this activity are in Student Data folder **Unit 5\Topic B**.

Here's how	Here's why
1 Open the Site Setup for Harvest-Valley-Market dialog box Update the Local Site Folder location to the current unit and topic	
2 Open index.html	In Design view.
3 Select the photograph	Market-tables.jpg is located to the left of the Welcome to Harvest Valley Market heading.
4 In the Property inspector, click the **Toggle Size Constrain** icon	(If necessary.) To lock the proportional aspect of the image.
Increase the Width of the image to **400** pixels	To dramatically increase the proportional size of the image. It now looks pixelated.
5 Click ⬛	The Sharpen button on the Property inspector. A warning box opens.
Click OK	(If necessary.) To close the warning box. The Sharpen dialog box opens.

6 Verify Preview is checked

    Drag the Sharpen slider to **1**   To apply the smallest level of sharpening to the image. Notice that the image is now less pixelated.

    Experiment with other Sharpen values   Watch the preview while you experiment.

    Set the Sharpen value to **1**

    Click OK   To accept the value and close the dialog box.

7 Click the **Reset to Original Size** icon

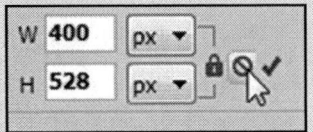

(To return the image to 227 by 300 pixels.) The sharpen value is still applied and has improved the overall clarity of the image.

8 Verify the photograph is selected

    Click   The Crop button. A warning box opens.

    Click OK   (If necessary.) To close the warning box.

    Observe the photograph

Crop handles are displayed around the image.

9   Experiment with the crop handles

Drag the crop handles as shown

Press (↵ ENTER)

10 Click ◑

Click OK

11 Verify Preview is checked

Experiment with the sliders

In the Brightness text box, enter **10**

In the Brightness text box, enter **-5**

Click OK

12 Save the file

Drag the handles until the part of the image you want to keep is surrounded.

To complete the crop, or press Enter.

(Or, double-click within the crop handles.) To complete the crop.

The Brightness and Contrast button. A warning box opens.

(If necessary.) To close the warning box. The Brightness/Contrast dialog box opens.

To watch how adjustments to Brightness and Contrast affect the photograph.

To slightly increase the brightness.

To slightly decrease the contrast.

To accept the value and close the dialog box.

External image editor

Explanation

Creating a relevant website requires graphics. Those graphics are designed in image-editing applications like Adobe Fireworks or Adobe Photoshop among others.

Since designing a website means you will be going back and forth between Dreamweaver and an external image editor on a regular basis, Dreamweaver provides a quick and easy way to do that by setting up a primary external editor. If you have more than one image-editing application installed, you can also set which file types an editor opens.

Adobe Fireworks

If Adobe Fireworks is installed on your computer, the pencil icon shown in Exhibit 5-3 becomes the Fireworks icon, and Fireworks is automatically set up as your primary external image editor. To seamlessly switch between Dreamweaver and Fireworks, select an image and click the Edit button in the Property inspector, as shown in Exhibit 5-4.

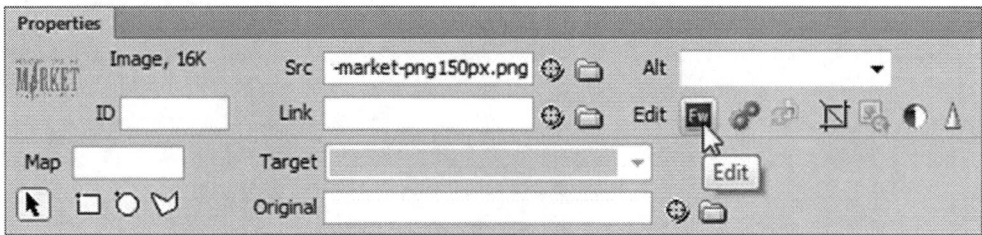

Exhibit 5-4: Edit button with Adobe Fireworks installed

Two other ways to open an image in Fireworks is to double-click the image file in the Files panel, or to right-click the image in the Document window and choose Edit With, Fireworks.

Set image editor by file types

If you have more than one image-editing application installed on your computer, you can make changes in Dreamweaver's Preferences dialog box so that specific file types will open the desired image editor. Here's how:

1 Choose Edit, Preferences to open the Preferences dialog box.
2 Under Category, select File Types / Editors.
3 Under Extensions, select a file type.
4 Under Editors, do one of the following:
   - Select one of the editors listed and click the Make Primary button.
   - To add an editor that isn't list, click the Add (+) button above the Editors list and navigate to the desired application and click Open. Verify the editor is selected in the Editors list and click the Make Primary button.
5 Repeat steps 3 and 4 for all the desired file types.
6 Click OK.

Dreamweaver will automatically use the primary editor for the file types you have set up. To use a secondary editor, right-click an image in the Document window and choose Edit With to display the submenu, and then, choose the desired image editor.

Do it!   **B-2:   (Optional) Editing images with an external image
                         editor**

The files for this activity are in Student Data folder **Unit 5\Topic B**.

Here's how	Here's why
1 Select the logo	At the top of the page.
2 Click [Fw]	(To open Fireworks.) If Fireworks is not installed and defined as the primary application for PNG files, the Edit button will have a pencil icon on it. The Find Source dialog box opens.
3 Observe the Find Source dialog box	If you had created this logo in Fireworks, you'd click Use a PNG to locate the original artwork file.
Click **Use This File**	To open the logo file in Fireworks.
4 Observe the Adobe Fireworks CS6 application window	You use this application to create and edit visual elements for your website.
5 Close Fireworks	And return to Dreamweaver. If prompted, don't save changes.
6 Choose **Edit**, **Preferences...**	To open the Preferences dialog box.
Under Category, select **File Types / Editors**	If necessary.
7 Under Extensions, select **.png**	If necesssary
Observe the Editors list	Fireworks is defined as the primary editor.
8 Click Cancel	To close the dialog box without making changes.
9 Close index.html	Without saving the file.

Topic C: Adding Flash

This topic covers the following Adobe ACE exam objectives for Dreamweaver CS6.

#	Objective
8.3	**Inserting Flash content**
8.3.1	Adding Flash animations and applications (SWF files)
8.3.2	Adding Flash video content (FLV files)

Working with multimedia files

Explanation

Dreamweaver makes it easy to add sound, video, and Flash files to your Web pages so that you can deliver content in ways that static text alone can't.

Flash content

You can insert Flash content in SWF or FLV format. If you insert a SWF file and it contains an embedded video, the file will have to download completely before a user can begin to view the video content. For this reason, SWF is best when the video has a small file size and short duration.

After you insert a SWF file, you can use the Property inspector to set its height and width on the page, adjust the video quality, set the animation to play automatically when the page loads, set it to play in a continuous loop, and apply styles to it.

To insert a SWF file:

1. Place the insertion point on the page and do either of the following to open the SWF dialog box:
   - Choose Insert, Media, Flash SWF.
   - On the Insert bar in the Media tab, click the Flash SWF button and select SWF.
2. Select a SWF file and click OK. A SWF placeholder is displayed on the page.
3. In the Property inspector, edit the file properties as needed.

When you save the page, a message appears, stating that two dependent files were created and saved in a Scripts folder in the site. These files are required for the Flash content to work, so it's critical that you upload the Scripts folder along with your other site files and folders.

After you have inserted a SWF file, you can view it by using Dreamweaver's Live view. First, though, you'll need to install the Flash Plug-in, using your primary browser, and then restart your computer.

Inserting FLV files

If you want to deliver Flash video (FLV files), you can choose streaming video or progressive downloading. If you want to deliver streaming video, you need a server running the Flash Media Server platform. When you stream video, the user doesn't have to wait until the entire file is downloaded. Streaming allows you to determine the bandwidth limitations of site visitors and deliver content accordingly. You can also provide additional interactivity, such as user controls, along with the video content.

If you deliver FLV content via progressive downloading, you do not need Flash Media Server. Progressive downloading has many of the same benefits of streaming, except for the bandwidth detection capability.

To insert an FLV file that downloads progressively:

1   Place the insertion point on the page and do either of the following to open the Insert FLV dialog box:

- Choose Insert, Media, Flash Video.
- On the Insert bar in the Media tab, click the Flash Video button and select FLV.

2   In the Video type list, select Progressive Download Video.

3   To the right of the URL text box, click Browse to open the Select FLV file dialog box, locate and select the FLV file, and click OK.

4   Set the desired options:

- In the **Skin** list, select the option that includes the tools you want included with the video.
- Click the **Detect Size** button to populate the Width and Height values.
- Check **Auto play** to have the video play when the page loads.
- Check **Auto rewind** to have the video go back to the beginning after playing.

5   Click OK.

To insert an FLV file that streams:

1   Open the Insert FLV dialog box, and in the Video type list, select Streaming Video.

2   In the Server URI text box, enter the file path for the Flash Media Server.

3   Set the desired options.

- In the **Stream name** text box, enter the FLV file name. The .flv extension is optional.
- In the **Skin** list, select the option that includes the tools you want included with the video.
- Click the **Detect Size** button to populate the Width and Height values.
- Check **Live video feed** if the video source is not a file but a video camera or webcam.
- Check **Auto play** to have the video play when the page loads when the connection is made with the server.
- Check **Auto rewind** to have the video go back to the beginning after playing.
- In the **Buffer time** text box, enter the number of seconds to buffer the video before attempting to play it. If Auto Play is checked, the buffer time is ignored.

4   Click OK.

Editing Flash content from within Dreamweaver

You can integrate other Adobe products with Dreamweaver to streamline your development process and workflow. For example, if you have both Flash and Dreamweaver installed, you can select any SWF placeholder in Dreamweaver and then click Edit in the Property inspector to edit the object in Flash. You can also right-click the SWF placeholder and choose Edit with Flash.

Do it!

C-1: Adding Flash

The files for this activity are in Student Data folder **Unit 5\Topic C**.

Here's how	Here's why
1 Open the Site Setup for Harvest-Valley-Market dialog box	
Update the Local Site Folder location to the current unit and topic	
2 Open vendor-booths.html	From the Files panel.
3 Place the insertion point to the left of the **Vendor Booths** heading	You'll embed a SWF file here.
4 Choose **Insert**, **Media**, **Flash SWF**	(To open the Select SWF dialog box.) You can also use the Flash SWF button that is located on the Insert bar in the Media tab.
5 Navigate to the media subfolder	
Double-click **HV-Market-ad.swf**	The Object Tag Accessibility Attributes dialog box appears.
6 In the Title box, enter **HVM Ad (Flash)**	To specify Alt text for users with screen readers and other assistive devices. When you embed media, it's important to indicate the file type in your Alt text.
Click **OK**	A Flash placeholder appears on the page.
7 In the Property inspector, click **Play**	To preview the Flash file.
Click **Stop**	In the Property inspector.
8 Save your changes	
Click **OK**	To copy the dependent files.
9 Observe the Files panel	(Click the Refresh button, if necessary.) Dreamweaver automatically created a Scripts folder to store the video's dependent files.

10 Close the file

11 Open vendors.html

12 Expand the **media** folder | In the Files panel.

Drag **Market.flv** to the blank line at the bottom of the page | (Drop the file above the orange line.) To open the Insert FLV dialog box.

13 Click Detect Size | To add the Width and Height values.

Check **Auto play** and **Auto rewind** | To play the video when the connection is made with the server and then rewind after it is finished playing.

14 Display the Skin list | To view the available options

Select the skin of your choice | Experiment by selecting a few different skins.

15 Click **OK** | To insert the placeholder.

16 Click Live | (To view the page.) The video plays automatically, and when it is finished, it rewinds to the beginning.

17 Return to Design view | Click the Live button again to deselect it.

Save and close the file

Topic D: Examining links

This topic covers the following Adobe ACE exam objectives for Dreamweaver CS6.

#	Objective
7.1	**Understanding basic link types**
7.1.1	Understanding that file:/// links are created in unsaved pages
7.1.2	Describing relative, absolute, named anchor, and email links
7.1.3	Targeting blank (_blank) to open a link in a new window

Hyperlinks

Explanation

Hyperlinks (usually called *links*) provide the functionality that makes the Web the interconnected world that it is. Links enable users to navigate to other pages in a site, to external pages and resources, and to specific sections of a page.

Link types

There are four types of links:

- *Local* links navigate to other pages and resources in a website.
- *External* links navigate to pages and resources outside a website.
- *Named-anchor* links navigate to specific sections of a web page. Named-anchor links are also called *bookmark links* or *intra-document links*.
- *Email* links launch the user's email client and a new message with a prefilled To email address when the user clicks the link.

Link targets

You can control how a link is opened in a browser. The instruction to a browser regarding where the link will open is known as the *target*. There are a number of different targets that you can use with your links. Link targets are typically needed in framed Web pages and pop-up windows. The possible targets are:

- `_blank` loads the linked document into a new unnamed browser window.
- `_parent` loads the linked document into the parent window of the frame that contains the link.
- `_self` loads the linked document into the same frame or window as the link. This target is the same as the default, so you usually don't have to specify it.
- `_top` loads the linked document into the full browser window, thereby removing all frames.

To specify a link target, select the text or image that serves as the link. Then, in the Property inspector, select an option from the Target list.

Link paths

Understanding the file path between the web page you're linking from and the document or asset you're linking to is essential to creating links. There are three types of link paths: absolute, document-relative, and root-relative.

Absolute path

Absolute paths provide the complete URL of the linked document, including the protocol to use (typically `http://` or `https://` for web pages), for example, `http://www.valleyharvestmarket.com/index.hml` is an absolute path to the file index.html. When you link to an external resource, use an absolute path.

Document-relative paths

Document-relative paths are usually best for local links in most websites. They're particularly useful when the current document and the linked document or asset are in the same folder and are likely to remain together. To make a document-relative path, your web page must be saved first. A `file:///` path is used until the page is saved.

If you're creating a link to a page or resource that's in the same folder as the page containing the link, you can simply type the file name in the Link box in the Property inspector. However, if the link destination resides in a different folder, you need to specify the folder name followed by a forward slash and then the file name; for example, `images/image1.gif`.

The forward slash always takes you down one level in the folder hierarchy. If you need to link to a page or resource in a folder that's up a level in the folder hierarchy, you use two dots and a forward slash; for example, `../images/image1.gif`.

Root-relative paths

Root–relative paths describe the path from the site's root folder to a document. You may want to use these paths if you are working on a large website that uses several servers, or one server that hosts several sites. With this method of link addressing, you always specify the path all the way back to the site's root folder. This method can be useful if you frequently move files. For example, if you have a page with a root-relative link and then move the page to a different folder, the link remains valid as long as the destination page or resource has not moved.

Root-relative paths must start with a forward slash, which represents the site's root folder. For example, `/harvestvalley/market/vendors.html` is a root–relative path to the file vendors.html, which is in the market folder in the site's root folder.

D-1: Discussing links

The files for this activity are in Student Data folder **Unit 5\Topic D**.

Here's how	Here's why

1 True or False: You can use an external link to navigate to another page within your website.

2 To control how a link is opened in a browser you use a(n) _____.

3 The following link is an example of a(n) _____ path.
   `/harvestvalley/market/vendors.html`

   When would you use this type of link?

4 The following link is an example of a(n) _____ path.
   `http://www.valleyharvestmarket.com/index.hml`

   When would you use this type of link?

5 The following link is an example of a(n) _____ path.
   `../images/image1.gif`

   When would you use this type of link?

6 When is a `file:///` path used?

Topic E: Adding links

This topic covers the following Adobe ACE exam objectives for Dreamweaver CS6.

#	Objective
7.2	**Creating links using the Property inspector**
7.2.1	Adding links: Link field, Point to File, or Browse for File
7.2.2	Adding a named anchor in the page
7.2.3	Identifying default text link formatting (blue and underlined)
7.2.4	Creating placeholder links with the # character

Creating links

Explanation

Because local links are links to pages and resources within a website, specifying the path is usually simple. If the destination file resides in the same directory (folder) as the page that contains the link, you can simply type the file name in the Link box in the Property inspector.

To create a local link:

1   Select the text or image that you want to serve as the link.

2   In the Property inspector, do one of the following:

- In the Link box, enter the name of the destination file. If the destination file is not in the same folder as the current page, enter the path and file name.

- Next to the Link box, drag the Point-to-File icon to the destination file in the Files panel.

- Next to the Link box, click the Browse for File button (the folder icon), locate and select the destination file, and click OK.

The preceding steps and options apply to any resource you link to, whether it's a web page or another resource type such as a PDF, Word or Excel file.

The anchor tag

Like any other elements, you can also create links manually in Code view. Links are defined by the `<a>` tag, which stands for anchor. The `href` attribute of this tag, which stands for hypertext reference, determines the destination of the link. Using a simple example, the code for a link to your home page might read as follows:

```
<a href="index.html">Home</a>
```

Link labels and link titles

Link text is sometimes called a *link label*; it should provide the user with a reasonable idea of what to expect when the link is clicked. For example, if you create a link for the text "download the menu in PDF format," that text provides sufficient information about the link, thereby enhancing the usability of the content. However, generic or out-of-context link labels such as "click here" or "this link," do not give the user an idea of what to expect if the link is clicked.

When your link text doesn't describe a link well enough, you can use a link title to provide more information about a link's destination page or resource. With the link text selected, enter a descriptive title in the Title box in the Property inspector. Screen readers also use link titles to provide context, which is an important aspect of Web site accessibility.

Do it!

E-1: Creating a link to a page in your site

The files for this activity are in Student Data folder **Unit 5\Topic E**.

Here's how	Here's why
1 Open the Site Setup for Harvest-Valley-Market dialog box	
Update the Local Site Folder location to the current unit and topic	
2 Open history.html	
3 In the top navigation bar, double-click **Home**	
	To select it. You'll create a link that navigates to the home page.
4 In the Property inspector, click **HTML**	(If necessary.) To display the HTML options.
In the Link box, enter **index.html**	To make the text "Home" a link to index.html. The file is in the same folder as the current page, so you don't need to specify the path.
Deselect the Home link	(Click anywhere on the page.) By default, links appear as blue, underlined text to distinguish link text from normal text. You can use CSS to customize link styles.
5 Save the file	

6	Open index.html	(From the Files panel.) You'll create a link on this page.
7	Double-click **History**	To select the text.
8	Make **History** a link to history.html	In the Property inspector, enter history.html in the Link box.
	Save index.html	
9	Preview the page in your browser	(Press F12.) To see the link in action.
	Click **History**	The browser navigates to history.html.
10	Click **Home**	The browser navigates to index.html.
	Close the browser	
11	Close the open files	

Named anchors

Explanation

By using *named anchors*, you can mark an element on a page as a target, and then create a link that navigates directly to that target. This technique is often used to make it easier to jump to specific sections on long pages. You can also link to a named anchor on another page in your site to take the user directly to specific content.

To create a named anchor:

1 From the Visual Aids list, select Invisible Elements (if it's not already active, as indicated by a checkmark) so that named anchor tags are displayed in the Document window.

2 Place the insertion point at the target location.

3 On the Insert bar in the Common tab, click the Named Anchor button to open the Named Anchor dialog box.

4 In the Anchor Name box, type a name for the anchor.

5 Click OK.

To link to a named anchor, select the text or image that will serve as the link. Then, in the Property inspector, do one of the following:

• In the Link box, type # (the number sign), followed immediately by the name of the anchor. For example: #*anchorName*.

• Drag the Point-to-File icon to the named anchor.

Do it!

E-2: Creating and linking to a named anchor

The files for this activity are in Student Data folder **Unit 5\Topic E**.

Here's how	Here's why
1 Open harvest-calendar.html	
2 On the Document toolbar, click [icon]	To display the Visual Aids list.
Verify that Invisible Elements is active	(There should be a checkmark next to it.) This visual aid will display symbols for named anchors.
3 Switch to Code view	You'll add an anchor at the top of the document. Switching to Code view sometimes makes it easier to place the insertion point in a precise location in the document structure.
Click to the right of `<body>`	``` 7 </head> 8 9 <body>| ``` At the top of the source code.

4 On the Insert bar, activate the Common tab and click the **Named Anchor** button	The Named Anchor dialog box appears.
In the Anchor Name box, type **top**	You'll create a link to this location in the document.
Click **OK**	(Or press Enter.) To insert the anchor.
5 Switch to Design view	
Deselect the anchor	
	(Click anywhere on the page.) To see the Named Anchor icon. This icon will not appear in a browser—it's displayed only in Design view.
6 Scroll to the bottom of the page and select the text **Go to Top**	You'll make this text a link to the *top* anchor.
In the Property inspector, in the Link box, enter **#top**	Links to named anchors start with the # sign.
Deselect the text	To view the link.
7 Save the file	
8 Preview the page in your browser	Press F12.
Scroll to the bottom of the page	To go to the view the Go to Top text.
Click **Go to Top**	To go back to the top of the page.
9 Close the browser	
10 Close the page	

External links and email links

Explanation

External links navigate to a page or resource on another Web site. To create an external link, you need to specify the complete address of the destination page or resource. You can also create an *e-mail link*, which starts the user's default e-mail program, begins an outgoing message, and inserts the specified e-mail address in the To field.

To create an external link:

1 Select the text or image that you want to serve as the link.

2 In the Link box, on the Property inspector, type the complete URL of the destination page or resource.

To create an email link:

1 Select the text or image that you want to serve as the link.

2 In the Link box, on the Property inspector, type `mailto:` followed by the recipient's email address.

Placeholder links

If you want to create a link but don't have the destination information available, you can create a placeholder link. Here's how:

1 Select the text or image that you want to serve as the link.

2 In the Link box, on the Property inspector, type a hash tag (#).

If the placeholder link was applied to text, the text will look and act like a link, meaning it is clickable, but it won't do anything. Be sure to update your placeholder links before going live with your website.

Do it!

E-3: Creating external links and email links

The files for this activity are in Student Data folder **Unit 5\Topic E**.

Here's how	Here's why
1 Open visiting-the-market.html	
2 Select **Rain or Shine!** text	
	(At the top of the page.) You'll make this text an external link.
3 In the Link box, enter **http://www.weather.com**	In the Property inspector.
In the Title box, enter **The Weather Channel**	To give users information about the link's destination.
Deselect the text	Since a CSS style is defining the link attributes, the only change to the text is the addition of an underline.

4 At the bottom of the page, select **email**

Getting help

If you have a question that [a]
market or send us an email.

You'll make this text an e-mail link.

In the Link box, enter **mailto:info@harvestvalleymarket.com**

When the user clicks the link, his or her default e-mail program will open, with this address used for the outgoing message.

5 Save the page

Preview the page in your browser

6 Click **email**

(At the bottom of the page.) An e-mail message with the specified address opens in the default e-mail application. (If no e-mail application is configured on the computer, you're prompted to configure one.)

Close the e-mail message

(If applicable.) Do not save the message.

7 Point to the **Rain or Shine!** link

To view the link title.

Click **Rain or Shine!**

To go to The Weather Channel's website.

Close the browser

8 In Dreamweaver, place the insertion point in **Rain or Shine!**

From the Target box, select **_blank**

Save your changes

9 Preview the page in your browser

Click the Rain or Shine! link

To go to The Weather Channel's website. This time, the page opens in a new browser tab.

10 Close the browser

11 Close visiting-the-market.html

Unit summary: Images, multimedia, and links

Topic A   In this topic, you explored the **GIF**, **JPEG**, and **PNG** file formats and learned how to insert those images, set image **attributes**, use **placeholders**, and create **rollovers**.

Topic B   In this topic, you learned how to use **basic editing tools** available on the Property inspector to make changes to images in Dreamweaver. You also learned how to access an **external image editor** from Dreamweaver, as well as define what image editor to use by file type.

Topic C   In this topic, you learned how to add and set the attributes for multimedia files that use the Flash **SWF** and **FLV** file format.

Topic D   In this topic, you explored the four **links types**, the various link **target** options, and types of link **paths**.

Topic E   In this topic, you learned how to **create links** to internal and external web pages, as well as how to use a **named anchor** and an **email link**. You also learned how to change the default link states by applying and editing CSS styles.

Review questions

1 The three main image formats supported by web browsers are ____, ____, and ____.

2 The following attribute for the `<img>` tag is required.

   A alt

   B height

   C src

   D width

3 Interactive buttons and tabs that change color when you point at them are examples of a(n) _____ image.

4 The Resample tool performs the following action.

   A Adds or subtracts pixels in an attempt to match the original appearance of a resized image.

   B Removes unwanted parts of an image.

   C Adjusts an image's highlights, shadows, and midtones.

5 True or False: If you insert a SWF file and it contains an embedded video, the file will start playing as soon as enough has downloaded.

6 True or False: Link targets control link formatting.

7 Use this type of path when creating links to external resources.

   A Absolute path

   B Document-relative path

   C Root-relative path

8 Use this type of path when creating links to local files.

   A Absolute path

   B Root-relative path

   C Document-relative path

9 Use this type of path when creating links for a website that uses several servers or hosts multiple sites.

   A Document-relative path

   B Root-relative path

   C Absolute path

10 By using a(n) _____ anchor, you can mark an element on a page as a target, and then create a link that navigates directly to that target.

Independent practice activity

In this activity, you will insert rollover images that include internal links, add and play a SWF file, and create an external link.

The files for this activity are in Student Data folder **Unit 5\Unit summary**.

1 In the Site Setup for Practice-Harvest-Valley-Market dialog box, update the Local Site Folder location to the current unit summary folder.

2 Open history.html.

3 In the first paragraph under the Our History heading, select **Springfield township** and create an external link to **http://www.townofspringfield.gov** with a link label that reads **Springfield Chamber of Commerce**.

4 In the blank paragraph at the bottom of the page (above the orange line), add a rollover image named **beets**. Use **beets.jpg** as the original image and **beets-colorized.jpg** as the rollover image. Preload the rollover image. Add **Beets are in season in June and July.** as the alternative text, and add a local link to **harvest-calendar.html**.

5 Click to the right of the image to place the insertion point.

6 Add five more rollover images using the information in the following table. Be sure to preload the rollover image, and add a local link to **harvest-calendar.html**.

Rollover name	Original image	Rollover image	Alt text
peaches	necterines.jpg	necterines-colorized.jpg	Peaches and nectarines are in season June thru Aug.
peppers	peppers.jpg	peppers-colorized.jpg	Peppers are in season July thru Sept.
rhubarb	rhubarb.jpg	rhubarb-colorized.jpg	Rhubarbs are in season July thru Sept.
squash	squash.jpg	squash-colorized.jpg	Squash are in season June thru Oct.
tomatoes	tomatoes.jpg	tomatoes-colorized.jpg	Tomatoes are in season June thru Sept.

7 Save the file and preview it in a browser. Test the rollovers and the links. If necessary, use the browser's Back button as you test the links.

8 Close history.html.

9 Open connect.html and add blank line at the bottom of the page.

10 Insert **market-nav.swf** with **HVM Nav** as the title. Use the options on the Property inspector to play the Flash file.

11 Save and close connect.html.

Unit 6

Working with code

Complete this unit, and you'll know how to:

A Understand the basics of HMTL, XHTML, and HTML5.

B Define a website's keywords and description in the `<head>` section.

C Use the Code Navigator and tag selector to select code element.

D Add and modify code in Code view by using options on the Coding toolbar.

E Use the Quick Tag Editor to add and edit HTML tags in Design view

F Use the Find and Replace dialog box to update content and code.

Topic A: Code basics

HTML

Explanation
As you already know, HTML code defines the basic structure of a web page. Even if you prefer to work in Design view, you should be familiar with basic HTML syntax.

HTML tags tell a browser how to interpret or display the content enclosed in the tag. For example, the `<h1>` tag identifies a line of text as a level-one heading, and the browser renders it accordingly.

HTML tags are enclosed in angle brackets: `< >`. Most HTML tags consist of a beginning tag and an ending tag. The ending tag includes a forward slash (`/`), which tells the browser that the tag instruction has ended. For example, the following code is a snippet of text that uses the `<b>` tag to define bold text:

```
Harvest Valley Market is open <b>Rain or Shine</b>.
```

A web browser would display this text as follows:

Harvest Valley Market is open **Rain or Shine**.

The following code shows the basic structure of an HTML document. Notice that some tags are nested inside other tags, and there's an ending tag for each starting tag.

```
<html>
  <head>
    <title>Document Title</title>
  </head>
  <body>
    All rendered HTML and content are inserted here.
  </body>
</html>
```

The standard tags that begin every HTML document are `<html>`, `<head>`, and `<body>`. The `<html>` element is considered the *root element,* or top-level element. All other HTML tags reside within the `<html>` tag. It defines the document as an HTML document. Every HTML document is then divided into two sections: the `<head>` section and the `<body>` section.

The `<head>` section contains the `<title>` element, which defines the document's title. This section also contains style sheet information, meta information, scripts, and other code or resources that aren't rendered on the page.

The `<body>` section contains all the content (text, images, etc.) that's rendered on a page, along with the code for it. Each tag in the `<body>` section performs a specific function to define the content.

The following table describes a few of the most commonly used HTML tags.

Tag	Description
`<a>`	Creates a hyperlink to another page or site.
`<div>`	Defines a section (division) of a page and allows all elements within that section to share formatting attributes.
`<span>`	Allows you to attach style attributes to an inline section of text, such as specific words or phrases within a paragraph.
`<table>`	Creates a table.

XHTML

XHTML is a more efficient and strict version of HTML. XHTML doesn't allow proprietary tags or attributes, the result is cleaner, more efficient code that is more evenly supported across different browsers. Dreamweaver CS6 builds web pages with XHTML code by default.

HTML5

HTML5development began in 2004 as a replacement for HTML 4.01, and will be concluded with the stable HTML5 Recommendation version which is expected by the end of 2014. The following lists some of the key benefits to HTML5:

- It is a single markup language that can be written in either HTML or XHTML syntax.
- It includes markup and Application Programming Interfaces (APIs) for complex web applications, which makes it a good solution for cross-platform mobile applications, such as smartphones and tablets.
- Adds new elements, such as `<video>`, `<audio>`, and `<canvas>`, that make it easy to add multimedia and graphics to a web page without having to use plugins.
- It is an alternative to Flash. In fact, Adobe is in the process of discontinuing development of the Flash file format for mobile devices and they have included the ability to create interactive HTML5 content in Flash Pro CS6.
- It is backwards compatible with older versions of HTML.
- It includes Web Forms 2.0.

Do it!

A-1:   Discussing code basics

Questions and answers
1   What are the standard tags that begin every HTML document?
2   True or False: HMTL5 is supplement to the current version of HMTL.
3   An ending tag includes a _____.
4   True or False: Dreamweaver CS6 builds web pages with XHTML code by default.
5   What is contained within the `<body>` section?

Topic B: Exploring head elements

Explanation

The `<head>` section of a web page contains resources for and information about the current document, such as a page title, keywords, scripts, internal style sheet rules, or a link to an external style sheet. The contents of a document's `<head>` section are never displayed in the browser.

Working with head elements

You can enter `<head>` section code directly in Code view, or you can use the Properties panel and the `<head>` section icons. The following table describes common `<head>` elements.

Item	Description
Meta tags	*Meta tags* provide information about the current document. For example, the `<keywords>` meta tag lists words that are relevant to the page's content and that are used by some search engines to help users find information. Similarly, the `<description>` meta tag is used by some search engines to categorize and summarize your site. Meta tags can also specify page properties, such as character encoding, the author, or copyright information.
Title	The `<title>` tag holds the text that appears in the browser's title bar. Search engines refer to a web page by its title.
Scripts	Scripts (usually JavaScript) may appear in the `<head>` section of pages that have dynamic content or functionality.
Reference links	The `<head>` section can include a link to files, such as external style sheets and scripts.
Style	The `<style>` section holds the CSS styles that constitute a page's internal style sheet.

Descriptions and keywords

Providing a description of your site (on your Home page) or of individual pages, as well as providing keywords, can be important to the site's effectiveness with search engines. When a search engine user submits search terms, search engines return a list of sites, usually listed according to the best match. Writing effective keywords and a page or site description can help improve your ranking in some search engines.

Descriptions can improve the overall quality of the search result. For example, Google and Yahoo use a site's description as the text that appears below a website's link in many search results. If a description isn't present, some search engines use the first text they encounter on the page, and this text might not be the first impression you want to make.

Because visitors often enter a site through its home page, it's common practice to provide a description and a list of keywords in the index (home) page. However, you can list keywords and descriptions for as many pages as you like.

Do it!

B-1: Discussing head elements

Questions and answers

1 Which elements might you want to include in the `<head>` section of your home page?

2 What are some benefits of using meta tags?

3 How can `<keyword>` meta tags help create more traffic to your site?

4 Where does the text in a `<title>` element appear?

Meta tag icons

Explanation

There are more than 30 types of meta tags. Dreamweaver can display a list of `<head>` elements as icons in the document window, as shown in Exhibit 6-1, below the Document toolbar. When you click a `<head>` element icon, its attributes appear in the Properties panel. To display a page's `<head>` content as a series of icons, choose View, Head Content or press Ctrl+Shift+H.

Exhibit 6-1: The Meta, Title, and Link icons in the document window

Do it!

B-2:   Examining a document's head section

The files for this activity are in Student Data folder **Unit 6\Topic B**.

Here's how	Here's why
1 Open the Site Setup for Harvest-Valley-Market dialog box Update the Local Site Folder to the current unit and topic	
2 Open index.html	You'll examine the elements in the `<head>` section.
3 Choose **View, Head Content**	To display the `<head>` section icons at the top of the document window.
4 Click 🗐	(The Meta icon.) To display the meta data in the document.
Observe the Properties panel	This page uses UTF-8 character set encoding, which stands for Universal Character Set Transformation Format 8 bit. Dreamweaver writes this tag into the page by default.
5 Click 🗐	(The Title icon.) To view the page title.
Observe the Properties panel	The title of this Web page is "Harvest Valley Market: Home."
6 Click 🗐	(The Link icon.) To display the style sheet linked to this page.
Observe the Properties panel	This page is linked to a style sheet named globalstyle.css. If the `<head>` section had multiple link resources, a separate icon would be displayed for each one.

Keywords

Explanation
Some search engines use meta-tag keywords and descriptions to help provide accurate search results.

To enter keywords:

1 Scan your pages and create a list of words that are relevant to your site's purpose and content. Include words that might not appear in your site's content but are likely to be entered by a user. For example, the word *recipes* doesn't appear in Harvest Valley Market website, but the word is relevant to the site and it's a word that users might enter in a search engine.

2 Choose Insert, Head, Keywords.

3 In the Keywords dialog box, type a list of keywords, separated by commas.

4 Click OK.

Do it!

B-3: Defining keywords for your site

Here's how	Here's why
1 Choose **Insert**, **Head**, **Keywords**	To open the Keywords dialog box.
2 In the Keywords box, enter **harvest valley, farmers market, organic, recipes, produce**	To create a list of relevant keywords that users are likely to enter in a search engine.
Click **OK**	To add the keywords.
3 Observe the `<head>` section of the document window	 A Keywords icon appears.
4 Click the Keywords icon	
Observe the Properties panel	The keywords appear in the Keywords box.
5 Save the page	

Descriptions

Explanation

Your site description should be a concise statement that describes the purpose or content of your site (or a specific page in the site). Most search engine users are looking for the best results as quickly as possible. Users are likely to skip over a long or poorly written description. Also, the search engine might display only the first line or two of the description.

To insert a description, choose Insert, Head, Description. Enter your description in the Description dialog box, and click OK.

Do it!

B-4:   Creating a description of your site

Here's how	Here's why
1 Choose **Insert**, **Head**, **Description**	To open the Description dialog box. You'll add a description that a search engine might use to index your site and display on a search results page.
2 In the Description box, enter **Harvest Valley Market is a farmers market providing locally grown, fresh food to Springfield, Missouri.** Click **OK**	
3 Observe the `<head>` section of the document window	A Description icon appears.
4 Click the Description icon Observe the Properties panel	The description appears in the Description box.
5 Switch to Split view Click the Description icon again	(If necessary.) The meta tag you created is highlighted. The `<meta>` tag uses the name attribute defined as "description" and the description text is defined by the content attribute.
Return to Design view	
6 Why is it important to write a concise statement as your site description?	
7 Save and close index.html	

Topic C: Selecting code

This topic covers the following Adobe ACE exam objectives for Dreamweaver CS6.

#	Objective
9.3	**Selecting specific code**
9.3.1	Working with the Code Navigator
9.3.2	Using the Tag selector to select tags in a nested hierarchy

The Code Navigator

Explanation

The Code Navigator provides a quick and easy way to view CSS files and rules that are applied to selected text or to where the insertion point is located.

You've probably already noticed the feature when working in Design view. As soon as your cursor or insertion point pauses for a few seconds, the Code Navigator icon appears as a ship's wheel. Click the icon to display the Code Navigator window, as shown in Exhibit 6-2.

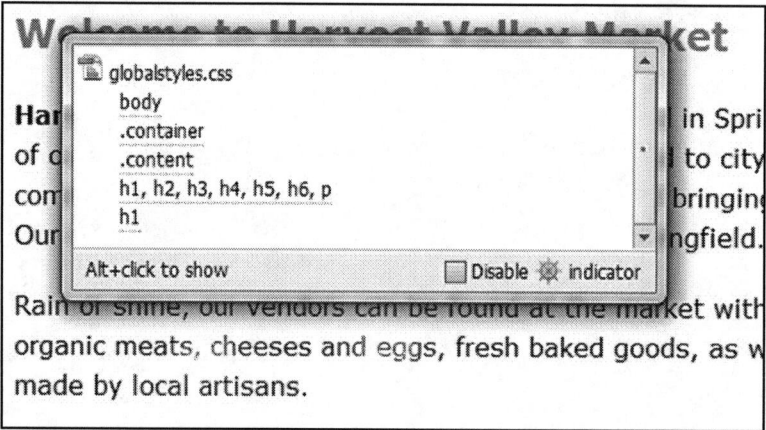

Exhibit 6-2: The Code Navigator window

Once the Code Navigator window is displayed, point to the CSS rules to view the declarations within the rule. Click on a rule to view the rule and its properties in the CSS Styles panel.

The Code Navigator icon is available in Design, Code, Split, and Live views. The wheel icon is also included on the Coding toolbar. Primarily this feature is used for CSS, but it also works for accessing JavaScript files from the `<script>` tag and server-side includes, as well as Dreamweaver templates and library items.

If you want to disable the wheel icon, display the Code Navigator window and check Disable. Click away from the window to close it.

The tag selector

You can use the tag selector to select a specific element and its contents. Depending on the current selection or location of the insertion point, the tag selector shows the parent tags, all the way back to the <body> element, as shown in Exhibit 6-3. The tag selector is located in the status bar at the bottom of the Document window.

```
<body> <div.container> <div.content> <table#specials> <tr> <td>
```

Exhibit 6-3: The tag selector, showing nested tags

Do it!   ## C-1:   Exploring the Code Navigator and tag selector

The files for this activity are in Student Data folder **Unit 6\Topic C**.

Here's how	Here's why
1 Open the Site Setup for Harvest-Valley-Market dialog box Update the Local Site Folder location to the current unit and topic	
2 Open index.html	
3 Place the insertion point in the H1 text and pause for a few seconds	**Welcome to Harvest** To display the Code Navigator icon.
Click the Code Navigator icon	To display the Code Navigator window, as shown in Exhibit 6-2.
4 In the Code Navigator window, point to **.container**	globalstyles.css body .container .con⊣ width: 960px; h1, h⊣ background-color: #FFF; h1 margin: 0 auto; Alt+click to show To view the declarations within the rule, which defines: a width of 960px, a white background color, and no margin.
Click **.container**	To display the rule and its properties in the CSS Styles panel.

5	Observe the CSS Styles panel	Under globalsytles.css, the class name you just clicked is selected and its proprieties are displayed.
	Observe the Document window	The Document window is switched to Split view, and the insertion point is in the code associated with the selected style rule.
6	Observe the status bar	(At the bottom of the Document window.) The left side of the status bar is blank.
7	Switch to Design view	
	Observe the status bar	The left side now contains the tag selector.
8	In the tag selector, click the `<body>` tag	

`<body>` `<div.container>`
`Properties`

		To select the tag and all the content with in it.
	Observe the Document window	The text, images, and table are all selected.
9	In the tag selector, click the `<div.container>` tag	The page has blue border around it to indicate that everything but what is contained in the `<head>` tag is selected.
10	Click the `<div.content>` tag	To select the content within the tag.
	Scroll down and observe the page	The "header" and "footer" content are not selected, but everything else is.
11	Click the `<h1>` tag	The "Welcome to Harvest Valley Market" heading is selected.
12	Close index.hml	Without saving changes.

Topic D: Inserting code

This topic covers the following Adobe ACE exam objectives for Dreamweaver CS6.

#	Objective
9.1	**Using the Code view of the Document window**
9.1.1	Using the Wrap Tag option to edit HTML source code
9.1.2	Collapsing and expanding selected sections of code
9.1.3	Applying and removing comments
9.1.4	Using code hints by typing <, /, or pressing the spacebar

Working with code

Explanation

Dreamweaver provides several tools for selecting and modifying code. In Code view, you can use the Coding toolbar to perform many common coding tasks.

The Coding toolbar

When you view a page in Code view, the Coding toolbar appears on the left side of the document window, as shown in Exhibit 6-4. You can use the Coding toolbar to perform tasks such as indenting code, expanding and collapsing code sections, and adding and removing comments.

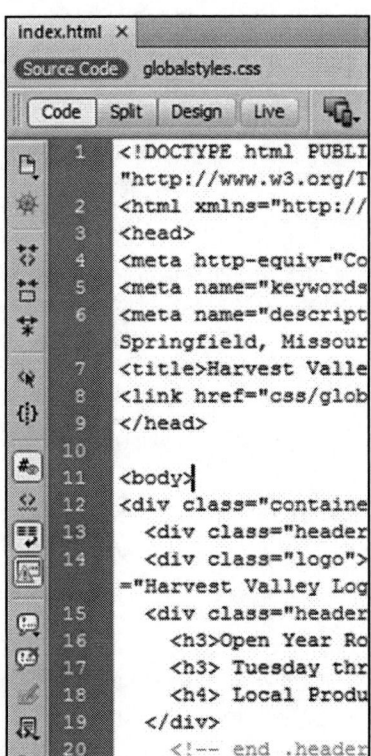

Exhibit 6-4: The Coding toolbar (on the leftmost edge of the Code view window)

The following table describes each of the buttons available on the Coding toolbar.

Name	Button	Description
Open Documents		Click to view a list of open documents.
Show Code Navigator		Click to display the Code Navigator window.
Collapse Full Tag		Place insertion point between a set of opening and ending tags and click to contract the code to a single line.
Collapse Selection		Select code and click to contract the selection to a single line.
Expand All		Click to restore all collapse code in the open document.
Select Parent Tag		Place insertion point in code and click to select the corresponding parent tag.
Balance Braces		Place insertion point in code that contains braces and click to select code from the opening brace to the ending brace. Also works with parentheses and brackets.
Line Numbers		Click to toggle on and off the vertical blue bar that contains the line numbers.
Highlight Invalid Code		Click to toggle on and off. When on, invalid HTML code is highlighted in yellow. Select the highlight to display the error explanation in the Property inspector.
Word Wrap		Click to toggle on and off. When on, horizontal scrolling isn't necessary.
Syntax Error Alerts in Info Bar		Click to toggle on and off. When on, syntax errors are displayed in an information bar at the top of the page and the line number is highlighted.
Apply Comment		Select text and click to display a list of five commands. Select a command to wrap the selection with desired comment tags.
Remove Comment		Select code and click to remove comment tags.
Wrap Tag		Select code and click to display the Quick Tag Editor.
Recent Snippets		Click to display a list of recently used code snippets.
Move or Convert CSS		Click to display a list with two commands: Convert Inline CSS to Rule and Move CSS Rule.
Indent Code		Select code and click to move it to the right.
Outdent Code		Select code and click to move it to the left.
Format Source Code		Select code and click to display a list of four commands: Apply Source Formatting, Apply Source Formatting to Selection, Code Format Settings, and Edit Tag Libraries.

Code comment tags

Comment tags are used to insert notes within the code on a web page. Here's how:

1   Select the text or code.

2   Click the Apply Comment button.

3   Select one of the following commands:

- **Apply HTML Comment** wraps the selection with < ! - - and - - >.If nothing is selected, a new tag opens.

- **Apply /* */ Comment** wraps the selection with /* and */. Use with CSS or JavaScript.

- **Apply // Comment** inserts // at the beginning of each line. If nothing is select, it inserts a single // tag at the insertion point. Use with CSS or JavaScript.

- **Apply ' Comment** inserts a single quotation mark at the beginning of each line of a Visual Basic script. If no code is selected, it inserts a single quotation mark at the insertion point.

- **Apply Server Comment** is used when you are working in a ASP, ASP.NET, JSP, PHP, or ColdFusion file.

Whatever is placed within the comment tags will be ignored by browsers, which makes it the ideal way to add notes to yourself and anyone else working on the code. A more advanced use is to isolate or disable sections of code when testing and troubleshooting.

To remove comment tags, select the code and click the Remove Comment button.

Do it!

D-1:   Inserting code and code comments in Code view

The files for this activity are in Student Data folder **Unit 6\Topic D**.

Here's how	Here's why
1 Open the Site Setup for Harvest-Valley-Market dialog box Update the Local Site Folder location to the current unit and topic	
2 Open index.html	
3 Switch to Code view	

4 Place the insertion point in line 29	
	`28     <h2>This Week's Specials`
	`29     <table id="specials">`
	`30       <tr>`
	
	To the right of the `<table id>` tag.

Click [icon]	(The Collapse Full Tag button). To collapse the all the line of code contained in the `<table>` tag into one line.

Observe the collapsed code	
	`28     <h2>This Week's Specials`
	`29 ⊞   <table ...`
	`61     <p> </p>`
	
	Lines 30 through 60 are now contracted into line 29. With the table code hidden, you don't have to scroll down as far to get to the end of the code.

5 On line 26, select **Harvest Valley Market**	
	`26 ⊟   <p> Harvest Valley Market`
	`       provide locally grown, fresh f`

Click [icon]	(The Wrap Tag button.) To display the Quick Tag Editor.

Type **b** and press ⏎ ENTER	
	`<div class="content">`
	`   <h1`
	`rvest` Wrap tag: `<b>`
	`   <p> Harvest Valley M`
	
	To add the `<b>` tag to the Quick Tag Editor.

Press ⏎ ENTER again	 `<p> <b>Harvest Valley Market</b>` To apply the opening and ending tags to the selected text.

6 Place the insertion point in line 12

```
11    <body>
12    <div class="container">|
13        <div class="header">
```

To the right of the `<div>` tag.

Click 🔲

To display a list of commands.

Select **Apply HTML Comment**

To insert the `<!--` and `-->` with the insertion point between them.

Type **.container defines the tag as 960px wide**

To add the comment text between the tags.

```
<!--.container defines the tag as 960px wide-->
```

7 Select the comment tag and text in line 67

```
66        <!-- end .footer --></div>
67 □    <!-- end .container --></div>
68    </body>
```

Observe how this comment is used

It defines the ending tag for the `<div class="container">` in line 12.

8 Click 🔲

To remove the comment tags.

Observe line 67

```
66        <!-- end .footer --></div>
67 □    end .container </div>
68    </body>
```

The tags have been removed but the text remains.

Press (CTRL)+(Z)

To undo the change.

9 Click **Highlight Invalid Code**

```
17            <h3> T
18            <h4> L
19        </div>
   Highlight Invalid Code  e
21            <div c
```

If necessary.

10 Place the insertion point in line 64 as shown

```
63    <div class="footer">
64        <p>&copy; |Harvest Valley
65        <p>This is a fictitious
```

To the left of "Harvest Valley Market."

Type **<** and observe

Dreamweaver lists the valid tags that you can use in this location as a hint.

Type **b>**

To complete the `<b>` tag.

11	On the Property inspector, click Refresh	To update the source code
	Observe the `<b>` tag	(In line 64.) It is highlighted in yellow because it is invalid.
12	Place the insertion point in the `<b>` tag	The highlighted tag.
	Observe the Property inspector	To see why the tag is invalid. It is marked as invalid because the tag is not closed.
13	After **Harvest Valley Market.**, type **</** and observe	The ending tag is automatically finished.
	Refresh the code	(On the Property inspector, click Refresh.) The invalid code hightlight is removed.
14	Click ⟺	(The Expand All button.) To restore the table content.
15	Return to Design view	
	Observe the **Harvest Valley Market** text	(In the first paragraph under the H1 and in the copyright statement.) Both are bold because you added the `<b>` tag.
16	Save and close index.html	

Topic E: Editing code

This topic covers the following Adobe ACE exam objectives for Dreamweaver CS6.

#	Objective
9.2	**Making changes to code using Design view of the Document window**
9.2.1	Using Quick Tag Editor to insert or wrap code around a tag
9.2.2	Right-clicking and choosing Edit Tag to invoke the dialog box

The Quick Tag Editor

Explanation

When you're working in Design view, you can use the Quick Tag Editor to add and edit HTML tags.

Insert an HTML tag

To insert an HTML tag:

1   Click on the page where you want to insert the tag.
2   Press Ctrl+T to open the Quick Tag Editor, as shown in Exhibit 6-5.
3   Begin typing and double-click the element in the list to insert it.
4   Add the element attributes, if necessary.
5   Press Enter to close the Quick Tag Editor and place the insertion point between the opening and ending tags.
6   Type to insert text inside the new HTML tag.

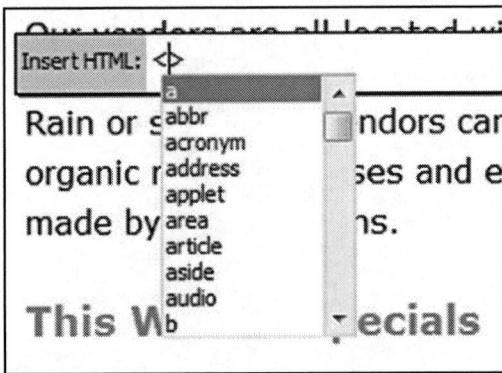

Exhibit 6-5: The Quick Tag Editor

Insert a Wrap tag

You can also use the Quick Tag Editor to wrap a tag around a selection:

1   Select the text and press Ctrl+T to open the Quick Tag Editor with the "Wrap tag:" prompt.
2   Begin typing and double-click the element in the list to insert it.
3   Add the element attributes, if necessary.
4   Press Enter to place opening and ending tags around the selection.

The Tag Editor

To open the Quick Tag Editor in edit mode:

1 Select an object and press Ctrl+T .

2 You can add or edit attributes as well as change the tag's name. To move from one attribute to another, press Tab to move forward and Shift+Tab to move back.

3 Press Enter to apply the changes.

You can also right click a tag in the tag selector and choose Quick Tag Editor to open the Tag Editor in edit mode.

Do it!

E-1: Editing code

The files for this activity are in Student Data folder **Unit 6\Topic E**.

Here's how	Here's why
1 Open the Site Setup for Harvest-Valley-Market dialog box Update the Local Site Folder location to the current unit and topic	
2 Open index.html Scroll to the bottom of the page	
3 Select the last line of text	Select "This is a fictitious market. All names and locations used in this website are fictional."
4 Press CTRL + T	To open the Quick Tag Editor with the "Wrap tag:" prompt.
Type **i**	 To highlight the <i> tag.
Press ↵ ENTER	(Or, click on "i".) To insert the tag into the Quick Tag Editor.
Press ↵ ENTER again	To apply the opening and ending tags to the selection

5 Deselect the text and observe the change

> In this instance, we are using the <i> tag to apply italic to the selection.

6 Place the insertion point in the last line of text

> When using this tag, it is recommended that you use a class attribute to describe the intended meaning and usage of it. Then if it is used more than once, you can distinguish one use from another.

7 On the tag selector, right-click <i> and select **Quick Tag Editor...**

> To open the Quick Tag editor in edit mode.

Place the insertion point between <i and >

Edit tag: <i>

8 Press (SPACEBAR) and type **class**

Press (↵ ENTER)

> To insert the class attribute and place the insertion point between the quotation marks.

9 Type **fictional website**

> To explain why you are applying the <i> tag to this text.

Press (↵ ENTER)

> To apply change.

10 Verify the last line of text is selected

Observe the tag selector

> The tag is listed as <i.fictional.website>. Dreamweaver adds a period between "fictional" and "website."

11 In Split view, observe line 65

> To view the tag and the class attribute.

12 Return to Design view

Save and close index.html

Topic F: Using Find and Replace

This topic covers the following Adobe ACE exam objectives for Dreamweaver CS6.

#	Objective
5.2	**Using Find and Replace**
5.2.1	Choosing search location (current page, folder, or entire site)
5.2.2	Choosing type of content to find (text, source code, or tag)
9.3	**Selecting specific code**
9.3.3	Using Find and Replace to find a specific tag

Find and Replace

Explanation

If you need to convert multiple instances of a particular word, phrase, or code, you can use the Find and Replace dialog box. Using Find and Replace can help you save time and prevent omissions. You can find and replace content and code within a single document, a selection, a specific folder, or an entire site.

To find and replace content or code:

1 Choose Edit, Find and Replace. (You can also press Ctrl + F.) The Find and Replace dialog box opens.

2 From the Find in list, select where you want to search. The options include Selected Text, Current Document, Open Documents, Folder, Selected Files in Site, and Entire Current Local Site.

3 From the Search list, select what type of content you are searching for. The options include:

- **Source Code** performs the search in Code view.
- **Text** ignores any HTML elements and searches for a specific text string.
- **Text (Advanced)** allows your search to focus on tags that are inside (or *not* inside) other HTML tags that you specify.
- **Specific Tag** searches for and replaces tags that contain specific attributes or attribute values.

4 In the Find box, enter the text or code you want to find.

5 In the Replace box, enter the replacement text or code.

6 Click Find Next. The first instance of the item you're looking for is selected (if it exists).

7 Click Replace to replace the selection with the replacement text or code.

8 Click Find Next to continue, click Replace All to replace all instances of the item, or click Close to close the dialog box.

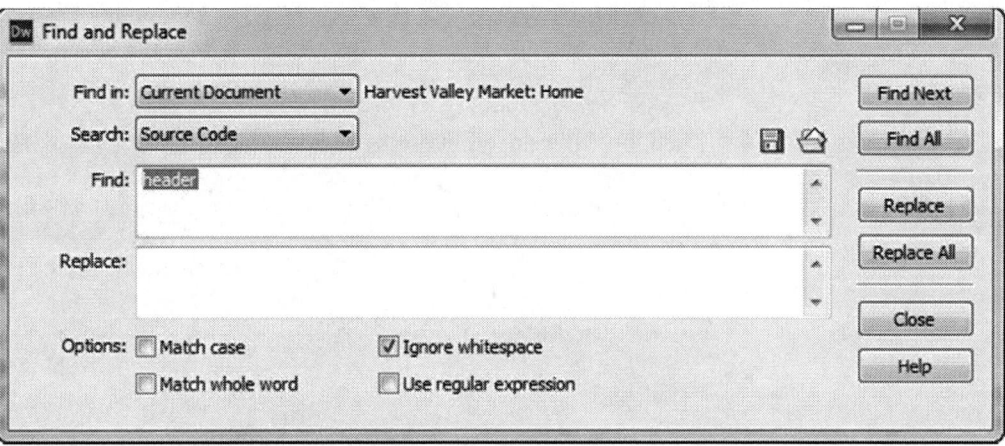

Exhibit 6-6: The Find and Replace dialog box

Do it!

F-1:   Using Find and Replace

The files for this activity are in Student Data folder **Unit 6\Topic F**.

Here's how	Here's why
1 Open the Site Setup for Harvest-Valley-Market dialog box Update the Local Site Folder location to the current unit and topic	
2 Open index.html	
3 Choose **Edit**, **Find and Replace...**	To open the Find and Replace dialog box. You'll replace the text "Copyright" with the code for the copyright symbol in every other page in the site.
From the Find in list, select **Entire Current Local Site**	
In the Search list, select **Source Code**	
4 In the Find box, type **Copyright**	
In the Replace box, type **©**	

5 Click **Find Next**	The connect.html page opens in Code view with the text "Copyright" selected.
Move the dialog box so that you can view the selection on the page	If necessary.
Click **Replace**	To replace the text with the character entity for the copyright symbol. The locations.html page opens with the search text selected.
6 Click **Replace All**	A dialog box opens, warning that this command cannot be undone in documents that are not currently open.
Click **Yes**	To replace all instances of the word "Copyright" with the code for the copyright symbol, in every document in the site. The bottom of the dialog box indicates the number of changes made.
7 Observe the Results panel	(At the bottom of the application window.) The Search tab is active, and displays a list of the replacements made in documents that are not currently open.
Right-click the **Search** tab	
Choose **Close Tab Group**	
8 Switch to Design view	
Scroll down to the bottom of the active page	(If necessary.) The copyright statement now begins with the copyright symbol.
9 Choose **File, Close All**	To close all open documents. A dialog box prompts you to save before closing.

Unit summary: Working with code

Topic A   In this topic, you discussed the basic structure of **HTML, XHTML,** and **HTML5.**

Topic B   In this topic, you explored what is contained within the `<head>` section. You also learned how to define **keywords** and a website's **description.**

Topic C   In this topic, you learned how to use the **Code Navigator** to access CSS files and rules. You also learned how to use the **tag selector** to select a specific element and its contents in Design view.

Topic D   In this topic, you worked in Code view and learned how to use options on the **Coding toolbar** to collapse and expand code, add and remove comments, and change the appearance of code as well as customize the coding environment.

Topic E   In this topic, you learned how to use the **Quick Tag Editor** in Design view to insert tags, wrap a tag around a selection, and edit existing tags with the Quick Tag editor in edit mode.

Topic F   In this topic, you learned how to use the **Find and Replace** tool to replace content and code. You learned that you can replace code in a document, a selection of text or code, a folder, or an entire Web site.

Review questions

1 The following are standard tags that begin every HTML document. [Select all that apply.]

    A <html>   D <body>

    B <head>   E <span>

    C <div>   F <table>

2 True or False: HTML is a more efficient and strict version of XHTML.

3 `<keywords>` and `<description>` are ____ tags.

4 To display a page's `<head>` content as a series of icons below the Document toolbar, press ____ + ____ + __ .

5 How do you disable the Code Navigator?

6 True or False: The tag selector is located on the status bar.

7 True or False: The Quick Tag Editor is only available in Design View.

Independent practice activity

In this activity, you will add keywords and a description, use the Code Navigator to select a CSS style that will be modified, collapse the content within a tag, add a comment tag, use the Quick Tag Editor to change a tag, and search and replace text.

The files for this activity are in Student Data folder **Unit 6\Unit summary**.

1 In the Site Setup for Practice-Harvest-Valley-Market dialog box, update the Local Site Folder location to the current unit summary folder.

2 Open index.html.

3 Add the following keywords to the website: **Springfield, Missouri, farmers, market, locally grown, fresh, fruits, vegetables, herbs, organic, meat, cheese, eggs, baked goods, local artisans.** (*Hint:* Start by choosing View, Head Content.)

4 Add the following description to the website: **Open Tuesday thru Saturday, 6am to 1pm year round with the best local produce, herbs, baked goods and organic meats that Springfield, Missouri has to offer.**

5 Place the insertion point in the table and open the Code Navigator window. Click **#specials** to open the style in the CSS Styles panel. Add the **background-color** property and apply **#FFC**.

6 Save globalstyles.css.

7 In Code view, view the Source Code and collapse the `<head>` tag.

8 In line 29, add an HTML comment that reads:
`<!--#specials defines the background color as #FFC-->`.

9 In Design view, place the insertion point in the **Open Year Round** text at the top of the page. Use the QuickTag Editor to change the tag to `<h4>`. (*Hint:* Right-click `<h3>` in the tag selector to open the QuickTag Editor.)

10 Use the Find and Replace dialog box to replace all instances of the Title text **Harvest Valley Market:** with **HVM:**. (*Hint:* From the Find in box, select Entire Current Local Site, and from the Search box, select Source.)

11 Save and close all open files.

Unit 7
Publishing

Complete this unit, and you'll know how to:

A Finalize a website to be published by checking download time, spelling, and links as well as cloaking files.

B Connect to a remote web server.

C Transfer local files to the remote server and use the Check In and Check Out feature.

Topic A: Performing pre-publishing checks

This topic covers the following Adobe ACE exam objectives for Dreamweaver CS6.

#	Objective
5.3	**Using Spell Check**
5.3.1	Accessing and running the Check Spelling command

Checking page size and download time

Explanation

Before you upload a site, it's important to verify that your page "weight" isn't excessive. *Page weight* is the total file size of a document and all the resources (images, movies, scripts, style sheets, etc.) that it loads when the page is requested by a visitor. The higher the page weight, the longer it takes to load the page. If your pages load slowly, some users (particularly those with slower connections) might leave your site and seek similar information or services elsewhere.

Dreamweaver calculates the size of an open document by counting up the kilobytes (K) of the document and all the resources that load along with it. The download time of a page at a particular connection speed is displayed in the status bar in the Document window.

Changing the download time baseline

By default, the connection speed in the status bar is set to 384K, which is a slow baseline by today's standards. You can change this setting in the Window Sizes category in the Preferences dialog box. The default you set should be based on an analysis of your target audience

Checking spelling

It's also important that you check for spelling errors and typos before you publish a site. To check spelling on a page, choose Commands, Check Spelling (or press Shift+F7).

Do it!

A-1: Checking page size, download time, and spelling

The files for this activity are in Student Data folder **Unit 7\Topic A**.

Here's how	Here's why
1 Open the Site Setup for Harvest-Valley-Market dialog box	
Update the Local Site Folder location to the current unit and topic	
2 Open index.html	

3	In the status bar, observe the page size and download time	This page's size is approximately 97K, and the page will take about 3 seconds to load. (This interval is based on the default assumption of a connection speed of approximately 384K.)
4	Choose **Edit**, **Preferences...**	To open the Preferences dialog box.
	In the Category list, select **Window Sizes**	To display the Windows sizes and the Connection speed options.
	From the Connection speed list, select **1500**	To set a faster connection speed as the target baseline. After conducting an audience analysis, you have determined that this is closer to the average speed with which your visitors access your site.
	Click **OK**	To close the dialog box.
5	Check the download time again	For users connecting at an average of approximately 1500K, the page will download in about 1 second.
6	How might you use this feature to help you create a successful site?	
7	Choose **Commands**, **Check Spelling**	To open the Spell Checking dialog box. The word "pm" is not recognized and the suggested replacement is "PM."
	Click **Change**	To make the change and keep checking. Next, Dreamweaver finds "lb."
8	Click **Ignore All**	To keep all instances of "lb." Check Spelling moves on to "doz."
	Click **Ignore All**	To keep all instances of "doz." No other spelling errors are found on this page.
	Click **OK**	To complete the spell check.
9	Observe the second line of text at the top of the page	You change "pm" to "PM" but left "am" alone. For consistency, you need to capitalize "am."
	Change **am** to **AM**	This is a good example of why you should never rely solely on Spell Check to proof your website.
10	Save and close the file	

Broken links and orphaned files

Explanation

Before you publish a Web site, you should verify that all of the links in the site work correctly. As you build pages, it's often easy to mistype a link or accidentally link to a page that was later deleted or renamed. If users click a broken link, the browser will display an error message indicating that the linked page cannot be found. Having to open each file and test every link would be a time-consuming and tedious development task. Fortunately, Dreamweaver can check the integrity of all of your local and external links for you.

To check links for an entire site:

1 Choose Site, Check Links Sitewide, or press Ctrl+F8. (You can also right-click in the Files panel and choose Check Links, Entire Local Site.) The Link Checker panel opens.

2 In the Link Checker panel, identify and repair broken links.

3 From the Show list, select External Links if you want to review the external links in the site.

4 From the Show list, select Orphaned Files to display any orphaned files that might exist in the site.

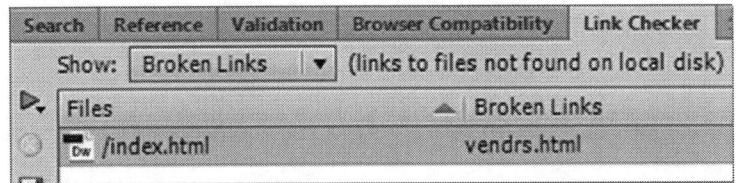

Exhibit 7-1: The Link Checker panel

Orphaned files

Orphaned files are files that reside in your site folders but have no pages linking to them. These files might include early drafts of Web pages or image files that you decided not to use. Removing orphaned files from your site before uploading prevents unnecessary bloat on the server and makes site maintenance easier. In the Link Checker panel, select Orphaned Files from the Show List.

Cloaking

Sometimes you might have orphaned files that you don't want to remove from the site. For example, you might have text documents or original image files, such as those in the Photoshop .psd format, that you might want to use later. Keeping them with the site folder makes them easier to find.

Cloaking folders or file types allows you to store them in your site, but prevents them from being included in normal site operations, such as link reports or uploading functions. To cloak a folder, right-click it and choose Cloaking, Cloak. Cloaked folders and documents appear with a red line through their icons, as shown in Exhibit 7-2.

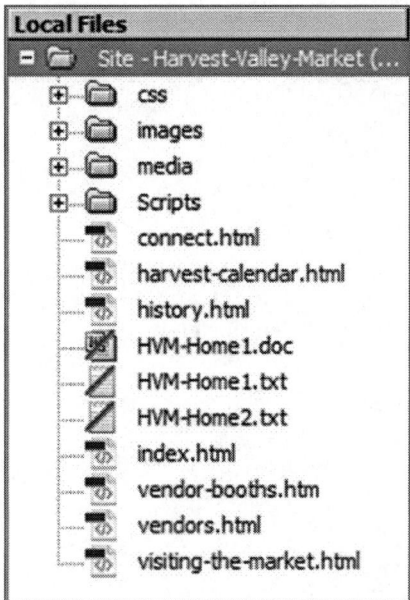

Exhibit 7-2: The Files panel, showing cloaked files

To cloak file types, right-click in the Files panel and choose Cloaking, Settings. In the Cloaking category in the Site Definition dialog box, check the Cloak files ending with box and then enter the file extensions you want to cloak.

Do it!   ## A-2:   Checking links and cloaking files

The files for this activity are in Student Data folder **Unit 7\Topic A**.

Here's how	Here's why
1 Verify no files are open	
2 Choose **Site**, **Check Links Sitewide**	The Link Checker opens at the bottom of the Document window.
Observe the results	The list shows that a broken link was found on the index.html page. In this case, a typo in the file name breaks the link.
3 Under Broken Links, click **vendrs.html**	You'll correct the misspelling of the file name.
Type **vendors.html**	To enter the correct file name for the linked file.
Press ⏎ ENTER	The file no longer appears in the list.
4 From the Show list, select **External Links**	To view the external links in this site's pages. These links don't indicate errors; they're listed for reference only.

5 From the Show list, select **Orphaned Files**	Several files appear that aren't linked to any pages in the site. You'll remove the image files. However, because you might need the text files later, you'll cloak those specific file types.
6 In the Files panel, expand the images folder	
Delete **pepper2.jpg**, **onions2.jpg** and **squash2.jpg**	Select each file and press Delete. You'll leave the other orphaned graphics in case they are needed later.
Collapse the images subfolder	
7 Right-click in the Files panel and choose **Cloaking, Settings...**	To open the Site Setup for Publishing dialog box.
8 Check **Cloak files ending with**	
9 Edit the box to include **.doc .txt** as shown	

> ☑ Cloak files ending with:
>
> .fla .psd .doc .txt

Click **Save**	A dialog box appears, stating that the cache for the site will be re-created.
Click **OK** and observe the Files panel	The three documents now have a red line across their icons, indicating that the files are cloaked and won't be uploaded with the rest of the site. They also won't appear in the list of orphaned files.
10 Right-click **Link Checker**	(Or any other tab in the panel.) To display a shortcut menu.
Choose **Close Tab Group**	

HTML validation

Explanation

Before you upload your site, you should also check to ensure that your code meets compliance standards. The World Wide Web Consortium (W3C) establishes coding standards. If your pages have code errors, the pages might be displayed incorrectly in certain browsers and alternative devices.

To validate the code for a page, open the page and choose File, Validate, Validate Current Document (W3C). The Validation panel opens with the results listed, as shown in Exhibit 7-3.

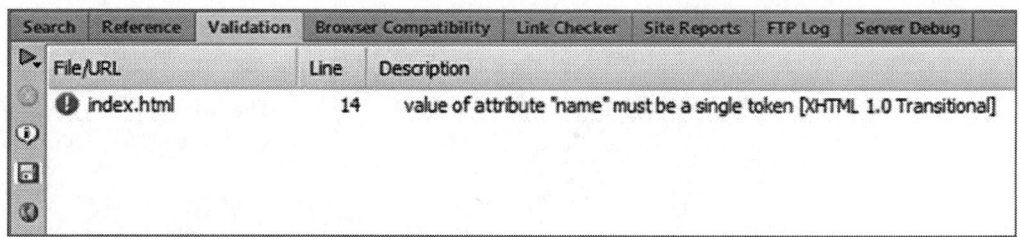

Exhibit 7-3: The Validation panel

To fix an error, double-click it in the Validation panel. The page that contains the error opens in Split view, and the offending code is highlighted. After fixing the code, re-check your code by clicking the green arrow icon on the left side of the panel and choose Validate Current Document (W3C). You can find additional information about the error by clicking the More Info button on the left side of the panel.

Sometimes an error's description might not be clear, or a single code error can produce multiple similar errors. If you see this error, it's often an extra closing tag. Double-click the first instance and correct the code—you'll often find that the number of errors in the list decreases.

To find additional information about W3C guidelines, you can visit the W3C site at http://www.w3.org. You can use this site to find information about changes or additions to the current guidelines and to find specific information about certain tags, such as which ones are deprecated. (A *deprecated* tag is one that is considered outdated; its use is discouraged in favor of new elements or CSS.)

Do it!

A-3:   Validating code

The files for this activity are in Student Data folder **Unit 7\Topic A**.

Here's how	Here's why
1 Open index.html	
2 Choose **File**, **Validate**, **Validate Current Document (W3C)**	The W3C Validator Notification window is displayed. Dreamweaver will connect to the W3C service.
Click **OK**	The Validation panel opens with one error.
3 Observe the error	The offending attribute value cannot include spaces. Instead, it must be one word ("token").
4 Double-click the error	Split view is activated, with the code error highlighted. In this case, the name attribute of the `<div>` tag.
5 Remove the spaces from **Harvest Valley Logo** as shown	
6 Click as shown	
Select **Validate Current Document (W3C)**	You'll validate the file again. The W3C Validator Notification window is displayed.
Click **OK**	The Validation panel opens with no errors.
7 In the upper-right corner of the Validation panel, click as shown	
Choose **Close Tab Group**	
8 Return to Design view	
Save and close the file	

Topic B: Specifying site connections

This topic covers the following Adobe ACE exam objectives for Dreamweaver CS6.

#	Objective
2.2	**Setting server information with hosting account details**
2.2.1	Adding new servers in the Site Setup dialog box
2.2.2	Understanding connection via FTP vs. Local/Network
2.2.3	Setting the root directory
2.2.4	Enabling Passive FTP when working behind a firewall
2.3	**Connecting via FTP**
2.3.1	Testing the FTP connection to verify settings are correct

Web site publishing

Explanation

When you are ready to publish your website, the most common scenario is that you'll copy the site files from your local PC to a remote Web server. A *Web server* is a computer configured with Web server software and the Internet protocols required to serve pages and other resources upon request. Dreamweaver makes it easy to set publishing parameters for your site and to transfer your site files to a Web server.

A Web server is connected to the Internet via an *Internet service provider* (ISP) or a hosting center. The ISP or hosting center provides space for Web site files, as well as other services such as site promotion and search engine optimization.

File names

How you name your files can be important based on the type of server that is hosting the site. For example, sites hosted on a UNIX server may require different file path protocols than other servers. Ask your organization's IT personnel for guidance on file naming conventions.

To create file names that comply with just about any operating system, follow these guidelines:

- Keep file names short. For ease of maintenance on the site, the file name should describe the file's content or function.
- Don't include spaces in the name. To separate words, use the underscore character or a dash; for example, `vendor-booths.html`.
- Always start file names with a letter.
- Treat uppercase and lowercase letters as separate characters. For example, your server might not consider `connect.html` and `Connect.html` to be the same file. A good way to keep from running into problems is to use only lowercase letters.

Server connection methods

Before you can upload your site files to a remote Web server, you must first establish a connection between your PC and the server. FTP (File Transfer Protocol) and SFTP (Secure File Transfer Protocol) are popular methods of transferring files. SFTP uses FTP, the standard file transfer protocol, and combines it with authentication and encryption protocols to protect the transmission.

WebDAV (Web-based Distributed Authoring and Versioning) is a set of extensions to the HTTP protocol that allow users to edit and manage files collaboratively on remote Web servers. Dreamweaver can also transfer data between servers located on a LAN (local area network), and transfer data by using Microsoft technologies such as the version control application VSS (Visual SourceSafe) and RDS (Remote Data Services).

Before setting up a server connection, check with your ISP or IT manager to make sure that the Web server supports the connection protocol you want to use. If it does, the ISP/IT manager typically provides the required information for connecting to the server, including the FTP host name, the host directory, and a login name and password.

Connecting to a remote server by using FTP

To connect Dreamweaver to a remote server for publishing files:

1   Choose Site, Manage Sites to open the Manage Sites dialog box.
2   Select the site you want to configure and click Edit. The Site Setup dialog box opens.
3   Click Servers.
4   Click the Add new Server button.
5   Type the name of the server.
6   Verify that FTP is selected, and enter the address in the FTP Address box.
7   Enter your user name and password for the FTP server.
8   Specify the root directory for uploading the site.
9   Expand More Options and check the following options if necessary:

  • **Use Passive FTP** to setup the FTP connection locally rather than having the remote server set it up. This is necessary when your computer is behind a firewall. If you are not sure if you should be using this option, test the FTP connection with it checked and unchecked.

  • **Use IPV6 Transfer Mode** to connect to an IPv6-enabled FTP server. Your ISP or hosting center will let you know if this is required.

  • **Use Proxy, as defined in Preferences** to specify a proxy host or proxy port. Consult your IT Administrator, ISP provider, or hosting center before using this option.

  • **Use FTP Performance optimization** to improve the transfer speed between your computer and the web server. If you have trouble connecting to your web server, uncheck and test the connection to determine if this option is causing the problem.

  • **Use alternative FTP move method** to use slower but more reliable transfer method. This option is only necessary when you connect to your web server but receive error messages when transferring files.

10 Click Test to test the connection.
11 Click Save to save the connection. The server name appears in the Site Setup dialog box. You can manage multiple site connections from this dialog box.

Connecting to a Local/Network server

If you are using a local web server or if your web server is part of your network, you won't be transferring files via FTP. Instead, you'll connect Dreamweaver using these steps:

1 Choose Site, Manage Sites to open the Manage Sites dialog box.
2 Select the site you want to configure and click Edit. The Site Setup dialog box opens.
3 Click Servers.
4 Click the Add new Server button.
5 Type the name of the server.
6 From the Connect using list, select Local/Network.
7 In the Server Folder, enter the file path or click the Browse button and navigate to the root directory on the web server.
8 Click Save to save the connection.

Do it!

B-1:   Setting up server connections

The files for this activity are in Student Data folder **Unit 7\Topic B**.

Here's how	Here's why
1 Open the Site Setup for Harvest-Valley-Market dialog box Update the Local Site Folder location to the current unit and topic Leave the Site Setup dialog box open	You'll explore the steps required to connect to a server through a secure FTP connection.
2 Click **Servers**	Site Setup for Harvest-Valley-Market Site Servers Version Control ▶ Advanced Settings If one or more Web servers were configured, they would be listed here.
Read the dialog box	
3 Click ➕	The Add new Server button is near the bottom of the dialog box.
Type **HVM FTP Server**	(In the Server Name box.) If you're making a new connection, this is where you'll type the server name.

4 Display the Connect using list and observe the options	FTP is selected by default. If the web server is local, you'd use the Local/Network option.
Verify that **FTP** is selected	FTP is an abbreviation for File Transfer Protocol.
5 In the FTP Address box, type **ftp.HarvestValleyMarket.com**	
	To specify the address of an FTP host where you will send files.
6 In the Username box, type your first name	In an actual situation, the server administrator would typically assign a user name.
In the Password box, type **password**	A server administrator would typically assign a password.
7 Observe the Root Directory folder	This is where you would specify the root directory for uploading the site.
8 Observe the Test button	When connecting to an actual web server, you'd click this button to verify the settings are correct.
9 Click **Cancel**	Normally, you would click Save and the server name would then appear in the list.
Click **Cancel**	To close the Site Setup dialog box.
Click **Done**	To close the Manage Sites dialog box.

Topic C: Transferring files

This topic covers the following Adobe ACE exam objectives for Dreamweaver CS6.

#	Objective
2.2	**Setting server information with hosting account details**
2.2.2	Understanding connection via FTP vs. Local/Network
12.1	**Transferring files by using Get and Put**
12.1.1	Understanding the difference between Get and Put
12.1.2	Choosing whether to upload dependent files
12.2	**Understanding and using Check In/Check Out**
12.2.1	Enabling Check In/Check Out in Advanced Site Setup dialog
12.2.2	Using Check In/Check Out to enable team collaboration
12.2.3	Overriding the Check Out feature to access locked files
12.3	**Uploading a site using the Files panel**
12.3.1	Understanding the differences between Remote and Local
12.3.2	Expanding and collapsing the Files panel to see both panes
12.3.3	Selecting the site's root folder to Put or Get the entire site

Site updating

Explanation

When you edit the content or design of a particular page, you can update that specific file on the Web server. Before updating a specific file, you might want to perform a *get:* download the version of the file that's currently on the Web server.

To get files from a Web server:

1 Connect to the remote site.

2 Download files or folders by using the following methods:

- To download an entire site, select the root site folder in the Files panel and then click the Get File(s) button.

- To download a specific file, select the file in the Files panel and then click the Get File(s) button.

Expanding the Files panel

After you have defined your remote server connection and connected to the server, you can expand the Files panel to display additional options for uploading a site, and to view both the local files and the remote folder you're publishing to.

Click the Expand button in the Files panel to expand it. The window is then divided into the Remote Server pane on the left, and the Local Files pane on the right.

To download a site to your computer, use one of these methods:

- To download an entire site, drag the root site folder from the Remote Server pane to the Local Files pane.
- To download a specific file from the site, drag the file from the Remote Server pane to the Local Files pane.

To *put* (upload) a specific file, select that file and click the Put files(s) button, or drag the file to the Remote Server pane.

Dependent files

When you get or put a file, Dreamweaver can prompt you to include that file's dependent files. *Dependent files* include assets and other files, such as images or style sheets, that are referenced by the file being put and that might have been altered or updated.

To enable or disable prompting, choose Edit, Preferences. Under Category, select Site. Check or clear the Dependent files options, depending on your preference.

Synchronization

Dreamweaver can synchronize your local and remote files by comparing the time stamps saved with each file. So, if you edit and save a page on the local site, it has a more recent time stamp than the version of that page on the server. To see which files are newer on the local site, right-click in the Files panel and choose Select, Newer Local. To see which files on the remote server are newer, choose Select, Newer Remote.

To synchronize the local and remote sites, do one of the following:

- Click the Synchronize with (server name) button.
- Right-click in the Files panel and choose Synchronize.
- Choose Site, Synchronize Sitewide.

Each of these commands opens the Synchronize Files dialog box, shown in Exhibit 7-4. Select synchronization options from the Synchronize and Direction lists, and click Preview. Dreamweaver then compares the time stamps of the two sites and updates the site containing the older files with the newer files. The Synchronize dialog box then appears, showing the file(s) that will be updated, and whether the action is a Put or Get. Click OK to complete the synchronization process.

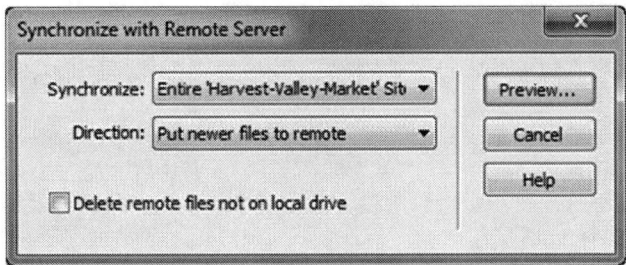

Exhibit 7-4: The Synchronize Files dialog box

Do it!

C-1: Using Get and Put to transfer files

The files for this activity are in Student Data folder **Unit 7\Topic C**.

Here's how	Here's why
1 Open the Site Setup for Harvest-Valley-Market dialog box	
Update the Local Site Folder location to the current unit and topic	
Leave the Site Setup dialog box open	
2 Click **Servers**	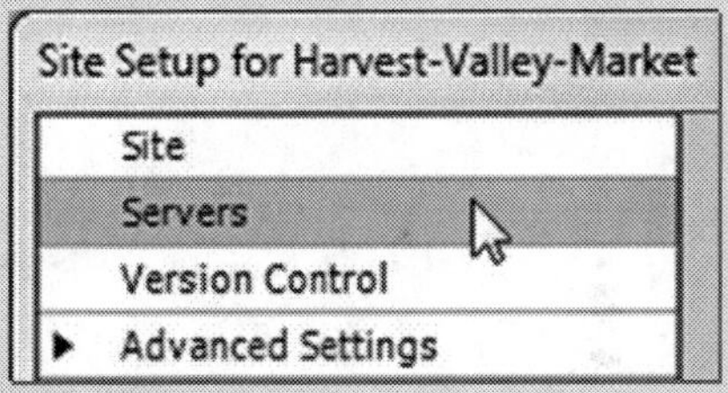
Click ➕	
3 Type **Test Publish**	
4 From the Connect using list, select **Local/Network**	Options related to Local/Network connections are displayed.
5 Next to Server Folder, click 🗁	
Navigate up one level, and open the **Test Site** folder	
Click **Select**	To specify the Test Site folder as the remote folder. You'll simulate uploading a Web site.

6 Click **Save**	The server name appears in the list. Dreamweaver recognizes it as a remote server even though the destination folder resides on your PC.
Click **Save**	To close the Site Setup dialog box.
Click **Done**	To close the Manage Sites dialog box.
7 In the Files panel, click [icon]	To expand the Files panel so that it shows the Local files pane on the right and the Remote Server pane on the left.
On the toolbar, click [icon]	(Or press F5.) To refresh the panel and display the remote folder. Because there's nothing in the folder yet, only the folder icon is displayed.
8 In the Local Files pane, select the Site folder	(The Site – Harvest-Valley-Market folder.) You'll upload the entire site.
9 Click [icon]	(The Put File(s) button.) To upload the site files from the local folder to the remote folder. A dialog box appears, asking if you're sure you want to put the entire site.
Click **OK**	To put (upload) the entire site to the "remote" folder.
Observe the folders in both panes	Both panes contain the same folders and files, except for the files you cloaked earlier.
10 Click [icon]	(The Collapse button.) To collapse the Files panel.

Check In/Check Out

If you're working with others to create a website, file version control can become a serious issue. To ensure that only one person can work on a file at a time and to avoid file version problems, use Dreamweaver's Check In/Check Out feature.

To setup the Check In/Check Out system for a website that is already associated with a web server:

1   Open the Site Setup dialog box.

2   In the left pane, select the Servers category.

3   In the right pane, verify the server name is selected and click the Edit existing Server button.

4   Click the Advanced button.

5   Check the Enable file check-out option.

6   Check the Check out files when opening option. With this feature turned on, you can double-click a file from the Files panel and check it out in one action. It is important to note that when you use the File, Open menu command the file isn't checked out.

7   In the Check-out Name box, enter your name.

8   In the Email Address box, enter your email address.

9   Click Save twice to return to the Manage Sites dialog box.

10 Click Done.

Check out a file

Once the Check In/Check Out feature is turned on, you can check out a file using one of these methods:

- Select a file in the Files Panel and click the Check Out File(s) button.
- If you checked the Check out files when opening box when setting up the Check In/Check Out feature, double-click a file in the Files Panel.
- Use the File, Open command to open a file without checking it out (assuming it hasn't been checked out previously), and then choose Site, Check Out.

After performing any of these methods, a dialog box opens asking if you want to include dependent files. Click Yes to check out the file and its dependent files, click No to check out only the selected file, or click Cancel to stop the check out process.

When you check out a file, a green check mark is displayed next to the file icon in the Files panel. If someone else checks out a file, a red check mark is displayed next to the file icon and the person's name is displayed.

Check in a file

Before you check in a file, save the changes and close it. Then, select the file in the Files panel and click the Check In button and you will be asked if you want to include the dependent files in the transfer.

After the file is checked in, the check mark is replaced with a lock symbol and the local version of the file becomes read-only. It is now ready for others to check out.

Override a checked out file

When a file is checked out, it is possible to override checked-out files by using an application other than Dreamweaver, such as a FTP client. When you view the remote directory in the FTP client, files that are checked out will have two versions listed: the normal file and a version that includes a .LCK extension. The LCK extension serves as a reminder that the file is checked-out and shouldn't be overwritten.

Do it!

C-2:   Using Check In and Check Out

The files for this activity are in Student Data folder **Unit 7\Topic C**.

Here's how	Here's why
1 Open the Site Setup dialog box for the current website	
Click **Servers**	
Double-click **Test Publish**	
	To display the Basic server settings.
2 Click **Advanced**	To display the Advanced server settings.
3 Check **Enable file check-out**	To turn on the feature.
Verify **Check out files when opening** is checked	When you double-click a file in the Files panel, it will automatically be checked out.
4 In the Check-out Name box, enter your name	
In the Email Address box, enter your first name and **@harvestvalleymarket.com**	To create an email address like *student@harvestvalleymarket.com*.
5 Click **Save** twice	To return to the Manage Sites dialog box.
Click **Done**	To complete the process

6 In the Files panel, double-click index.html	To open the file and check it out. A dialog opens asking if you want to include dependent files.
Click **No**	You will not be making changes to the dependent files, so checking them out isn't necessary.
7 Observe index.html in the Files panel	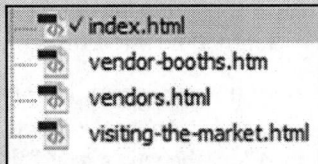
	Index.html has a green check mark to the right of the file icon. This means that you have the file checked out. When another contributor has the file checked out, the check mark is red.
8 In the first line of text under the H1 heading, select **Missouri**	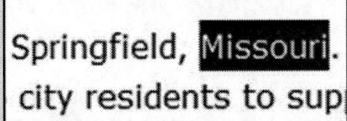
Enter **MO**	To replace the state name with its abberviation.
Save and close the file	
9 Click 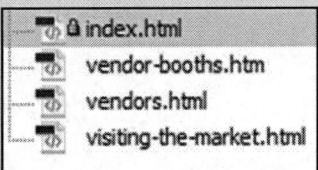	(The Check In button.) To check in the file and automatically update it on the server. A dialog box opens asking if you want to include the dependent files.
Click **No**	Since you didn't check them out.
10 Observe index.html in the Files panel	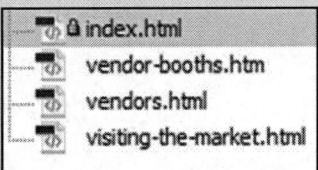
	The green check mark is replaced with a lock icon.
11 Close any open files	If necessary.

Unit summary: Publishing

Topic A   In this topic, you learned how to prepare a website to be published by checking **file size** and download time as well as checking spelling. Next, you learned how to find and fix **broken links** and **orphaned files**. You also learned how to validate code.

Topic B   In this topic, learned the basics of **website publishing** with Dreamweaver. You also learned how to **connect to a server** using FTP.

Topic C   In this topic, you learned how to **upload local files** to a remote site using the Files panel. You also learned how to expand and collapse the Files panel. You learned to select the site's root folder and then use **Put** or **Get** to upload or download the entire site. Finally, you learned how to use the **Check In** and **Check Out** feature to avoid file version control problems.

Review questions

1 How can you change the connection speed with which Dreamweaver calculates download time?

A Select a new connection speed from the Page Size/DownloadTtime list in the status bar.

B Right-click the Page Size/Download Time list in the status bar and choose a new connection speed.

C Open the Page Properties dialog box, select the Title/Encoding category, and select a new connection speed from the Connection speed list.

D Open the Preferences dialog box, select the Windows Sizes category, and select a new connection speed from the Connection speed list.

2 How can you check links site-wide? [Choose all that apply.]

A Press Ctrl+F8.

B Right-click the Files panel and choose Check Links, Entire Local Site.

C Choose Site, Check Links Sitewide.

D Select a file in the Files panel, and click Check Links Sitewide in the Property inspector.

3 How can you cloak specific file types?

A In the Files panel, right-click a file that you want to cloak and choose Cloak File Type.

B Open the Preferences dialog box and select the File Types/Editors category. Check "Cloak files ending with" and enter the file extensions you want to cloak.

C Right-click the Files panel and choose Cloaking, Settings. In the Cloaking category, check "Cloak files ending with" and enter the file extensions you want to cloak.

D Choose Site, Advanced, Cloak Files Ending With. In the dialog box, enter the file extensions you want to cloak.

4 Which of the following are general guidelines to consider when you're naming site files? [Choose all that apply.]

   A Keep file names as short and meaningful as possible.

   B Start file names with a number.

   C Start file names with a letter.

   D Don't include spaces in the file names.

   E Separate words in the file names with one space only.

5 True or False: When you are setting up an FTP connection, check the Use Passive FTP option when your computer is behind a firewall.

6 True or False: After checking in a file, a lock symbol appears next to the file name in the Files panel and the local file is editable.

7 Which of the following are ways you can connect to a server?
   [Choose all that apply.]

   A FTP

   B SFTP

   C XML

   D WebDAV

8 How can you synchronize local and remote site files?
   [Choose all that apply.]

   A Choose Site, Synchronize.

   B In the Files panel, click the Refresh button.

   C Choose File, Check Page, Check Accessibility.

   D Right-click in the Files panel and choose Synchronize.

   E Click the "Synchronize with (server name)" button.

9 After you connect to a remote server, how can you upload an individual file?
   [Choose all that apply.]

   A Select the file in the Files panel and click the Put File(s) button.

   B In the Files panel, select the folder containing the file and click the Put File(s) button.

   C Expand the Files panel, and drag the folder containing the file from the Local Files pane to the Remote Site pane.

   D Expand the Files panel, and drag the file from the Local Files pane to the appropriate folder in the Remote Server pane.

Independent practice activity

In this activity, you'll spell check a Web site, check for broken links and orphaned files, and practice uploading a Web site by uploading it to a local folder.

The files for this activity are in Student Data folder **Unit 7\Unit summary**.

1 In the Site Setup for Practice-Harvest-Valley-Market dialog box, update the Local Site Folder location to the current unit summary folder.

2 Spell check all the HTML files. Use your judgment to determine if an error needs to be corrected or not. (*Hint:* open a file and press Shift + F7.)

3 Check the links in the site. (*Hint:* In the Files panel, right-click the site and choose Check Links, Entire Local Site.)

4 Repair the broken link that was caused by a typographic error, and run the Link Checker again.

5 Check the external links and the orphaned files.

6 Establish a Local/Network connection to the Test Site folder in the Unit summary folder named **Practice Test Server**. (*Hint:* In the Site Setup dialog box, use the options in the Servers category.)

7 View both the local files and the remote Test Site folder. (*Hint:* Expand the Files panel.)

8 Upload the entire site to the Test Site folder. (*Hint:* In the Local Files pane, select the Site folder and then click the Put File(s) button.)

9 Collapse the Files panel, and close Dreamweaver.

Appendix A
ACE exam objectives map

This appendix covers these additional topics:

A ACE exam objectives for Dreamweaver CS6, with references to corresponding coverage in ILT Series courseware.

Topic A: Comprehensive exam objectives

Explanation
The following table lists the Adobe Certified Expert (ACE) exam objectives for Dreamweaver CS6 and indicates where each objective is covered in conceptual explanations, hands-on activities, or both.

1 Navigating the workspace

#	Objective	Course level	Conceptual information	Supporting activities
1.1	**Working with the Document window**			
1.1.1	Understanding Code view, Split view, and Design view	Basic	Unit 1, Topic C	C-1
1.1.2	Adding a Title in the Title field (where it appears and why)	Basic	Unit 1, Topic C	C-3
1.1.3	Difference between enabling Live View and Live Code	Basic	Unit 1, Topic C	C-2
1.1.4	Refreshing Design view after updating code	Basic	Unit 1, Topic C	C-3
1.2	**Managing files in the Files panel**			
1.2.1	Understanding how to configure Files panel to sort files.	Basic	Unit 2, Topic D	D-1
1.2.2	Using the options in the Files panel to choose/manage sites.	Basic	Unit 2, Topic D	D-1
1.3	**Updating properties in the Property inspector**			
1.3.1	Setting contextual options to affect selected elements	Basic	Unit 1, Topic D	D-1
1.3.2	Understanding HTML vs. CSS sections of Property inspector	Basic	Unit 1, Topic D	D-1
		Basic	Unit 4, Topic C	C-1, C-3
1.4	**Configure workspace layout**			
1.4.1	Applying the pre-configured workspace layouts	Basic	Unit 1, Topic B	B-2
1.4.2	Customizing personalized workspace layouts	Basic	Unit 1, Topic B	B-4

2 Defining a site

#	Objective	Course level	Conceptual information	Supporting activities
2.1	**Creating the local root folder**			
2.1.1	Understanding the concept of the site's local root folder	Basic	Unit 2, Topic B	B-1
2.2	**Setting server information with hosting account details**			
2.2.1	Adding new servers in the Site Setup dialog box	Basic	Unit 7, Topic B	B-1
2.2.2	Understanding connection via FTP vs. Local/Network	Basic	Unit 7, Topic B	B-1
		Basic	Unit 7, Topic C	C-1
2.2.3	Setting the root directory	Basic	Unit 7, Topic B	B-1
2.2.4	Enabling Passive FTP when working behind a firewall	Basic	Unit 7, Topic B	
2.3	**Connecting via FTP**			
2.3.1	Testing the FTP connection to verify settings are correct	Basic	Unit 7, Topic B	B-1

3 Creating Web pages

#	Objective	Course level	Conceptual information	Supporting activities
3.1	**Using the New Document dialog box**			
3.1.1	Describing the basic file types Dreamweaver can create	Basic	Unit2, Topic C	C-1
3.1.2	Setting the default page extension preference (.html or .htm)	Basic	Unit 2, Topic C	C-2
3.2	**Creating and managing files with the Files panel**			
3.2.1	Understanding why pages must be saved in local root folder	Basic	Unit 2, Topic E	
3.2.2	Organizing the hierarchy of files/folders to create site map	Basic	Unit 2, Topic E	
3.2.3	Repositioning pages in the Files panel prevents broken links	Basic	Unit 2, Topic E	E-1

#	Objective	Course level	Conceptual information	Supporting activities
3.3	**Previewing pages in a browser**			
3.3.1	Setting the primary and secondary browsers	Basic	Unit 1, Topic E	E-2
3.3.2	Understanding the advantages of testing pages in a browser	Basic	Unit 1, Topic E	

4 Laying out pages

#	Objective	Course level	Conceptual information	Supporting activities
4.1	**Using the Layout section of the Insert panel**			
4.1.1	Understanding Div containers vs. AP Divs	Advanced	Unit 1, Topic B	B-1
		Advanced	Unit 2, Topic A	A-1
		Advanced	Unit 2, Topic B	B-1
4.1.2	Nesting Div containers	Advanced	Unit 1, Topic A	A-2
4.1.3	Describing behavior of Div containers (expand to fit content)	Advanced	Unit 1, Topic A	A-1
		Advanced	Unit 1, Topic B	
4.1.4	Advantages of Div containers vs. using table cell layouts	Advanced	Unit 1, Topic A	
		Advanced	Unit 4, Topic C	
4.2	**Creating fluid grid layouts**			
4.2.1	Benefits of creating a fluid layout that targets 3 resolutions	Advanced	Unit 1, Topic C	
4.2.2	Using the Insert panel to add new Fluid Grid Div containers	Advanced	Unit 1, Topic C	C-2
4.2.3	Enabling Live View to define page region Div containers	Advanced	Unit 1, Topic B	B-4
4.2.4	Using the Resolution Switcher to set/view each resolution	Advanced	Unit 1, Topic C	C-1
4.2.5	Using the Multiscreen Preview panel to view simultaneously	Advanced	Unit 1, Topic C	C-4

5 Adding and formatting text

#	Objective	Course level	Conceptual information	Supporting activities
5.1	**Inserting special characters**			
5.1.1	Describing situations that require inserting special characters	Basic	Unit 3, Topic B	
5.1.2	Understanding HTML encoding used for special characters	Basic	Unit 3, Topic B	B-1
5.2	**Using Find and Replace**			
5.2.1	Choosing search location (current page, folder, or entire site)	Basic	Unit 6, Topic F	F-1
5.2.2	Choosing type of content to find (text, source code, or tag)	Basic	Unit 6, Topic F	F-1
5.3	**Using Spell Check**			
5.3.1	Accessing and running the Check Spelling command	Basic	Unit 7, Topic A	A-1
5.4	**Understanding paragraph and header tags**			
5.4.1	Benefits of using the appropriate tags to contain text content	Basic	Unit 3, Topic C	C-1
5.4.2	Setting text format (P, H1, etc.) in the Property inspector	Basic	Unit 3, Topic C	C-1
5.5	**Inserting line breaks**			
5.5.1	Understanding the difference between <p> and tags	Basic	Unit 3, Topic D	D-1
5.6	**Creating lists**			
5.6.1	Understanding 3 types of lists: bullet, numbered, definition	Basic	Unit 3, Topic E	E-1
5.6.2	Indenting list items in the Property inspector	Basic	Unit 3, Topic E	E-1

6 Working with Cascading Style Sheets (CSS)

#	Objective	Course level	Conceptual information	Supporting activities
6.1	**Understanding basic CSS syntax**			
6.1.1	Describing 4 main selectors (Class, ID, Tag, and Compound)	Basic	Unit 4, Topic A	
6.1.2	Describing 3 locations for CSS (inline, HTML head, external)	Basic	Unit 4, Topic A	
		Basic	Unit 4, Topic B	B-1
6.1.3	Understanding the cascade effect (which rules are applied)	Basic	Unit 4, Topic D	D-1
		Advanced	Unit 1, Topic A	A-1
6.1.4	Understanding that CSS rules specify properties of elements	Basic	Unit 4, Topic A	
		Basic	Unit 4, Topic B	B-1
		Advanced	Unit 1, Topic A	A-1
6.1.5	Understanding that CSS can format and position page items	Basic	Unit 4, Topic A	
		Basic	Unit 4, Topic B	B-1
		Advanced	Unit 2, Topic A	
6.1.6	Understanding the difference between margin and padding	Basic	Unit 2, Topic C	C-3
		Advanced	Unit 1, Topic B	B-2
6.1.7	Setting color properties with hexadecimal values	Basic	Unit 2, Topic C	C-3
		Basic	Unit 4, Topic B	B-1
6.1.8	Using common CSS measurement values (%, pixel, and em)	Basic	Unit 4, Topic C	C-1
		Advanced	Unit 1, Topic B	
6.2	**Creating and managing CSS styles in the CSS Styles panel**			
6.2.1	Linking an external CSS style sheet to a Web page	Basic	Unit 4, Topic B	
		Advanced	Unit 1, Topic A	A-2
6.2.2	Creating a new CSS style in the panel	Basic	Unit 4, Topic B	B-1
		Advanced	Unit 1, Topic B	B-3
6.2.3	Editing a CSS style in the CSS Rule Definition dialog box	Basic	Unit 4, Topic C	C-2
		Advanced	Unit 1, Topic B	B-2
6.2.4	Adding and deleting rules in the Properties pane	Basic	Unit 4, Topic C	C-1, C-3

#	Objective	Course level	Conceptual information	Supporting activities
6.3	**Applying styles using the Property inspector**			
6.3.1	Applying a style using the Target Rule list in the CSS section	Basic	Unit 4, Topic C	C-3
6.3.2	Using the Edit Style option in the CSS section	Basic	Unit 4, Topic C	
6.3.3	Setting the Class of a selected element in the HTML section	Basic	Unit 4, Topic C	C-2
6.3.4	Setting the ID of a selected element in the HTML section	Basic	Unit 4, Topic A	
		Advanced	Unit 1, Topic B	B-2

7 Adding and managing links

#	Objective	Course level	Conceptual information	Supporting activities
7.1	**Understanding basic link types**			
7.1.1	Understanding that file:/// links are created in unsaved pages	Basic	Unit 5, Topic D	D-1
7.1.2	Describing relative, absolute, named anchor, and email links	Basic	Unit 5, Topic D	D-1
7.1.3	Targeting blank (_blank) to open a link in a new window	Basic	Unit 5, Topic D	D-1
7.2	**Creating links using the Property inspector**			
7.2.1	Adding links: Link field, Point to File, or Browse for File	Basic	Unit 5, Topic E	E-1
7.2.2	Adding a named anchor in the page	Basic	Unit 5, Topic E	E-2
7.2.3	Identifying default text link formatting (blue and underlined)	Basic	Unit 5, Topic E	E-1
7.2.4	Creating placeholder links with the # character	Basic	Unit 5, Topic E	
7.3	**Creating content navigation**			
7.3.1	Understanding how to insert Spry Layout Objects (widgets)	Advanced	Unit 4, Topic B	B-1
7.3.2	Adding/deleting menu items and panels in the Property inspector	Advanced	Unit 4, Topic B	B-1
7.3.3	Reordering menu items and panels in the Property inspector	Advanced	Unit 4, Topic B	B-1

8 Adding images and rich media

#	Objective	Course level	Conceptual information	Supporting activities
8.1	**Inserting images**			
8.1.1	Requirement of saving image files in the local root folder	Basic	Unit 5, Topic A	
8.1.2	Inserting placeholder images while designing a site	Basic	Unit 5, Topic A	A-4
8.1.3	Inserting rollover images	Basic	Unit 5, Topic A	A-5
8.1.4	Benefits of adding Alternate text for SEO and accessibility	Basic	Unit 5, Topic A	
8.1.5	Setting Align property to wrap images in the text containers	Advanced	Unit 1, Topic B	B-3
8.1.6	Understanding images should be at original size (don't scale)	Basic	Unit 5, Topic A	A-3
8.2	**Using the Property inspector to update and edit images**			
8.2.1	Understanding the crop, sharpen, brightness/contrast tools	Basic	Unit 5, Topic B	B-1
8.2.2	Using round-trip editing to launch external image editors	Basic	Unit 5, Topic B	B-2
8.3	**Inserting Flash content**			
8.3.1	Adding Flash animations and applications (SWF files)	Basic	Unit 5, Topic C	C-1
8.3.2	Adding Flash video content (FLV files)	Basic	Unit 5, Topic C	C-1

9 Writing HTML code

#	Objective	Course level	Conceptual information	Supporting activities
9.1	**Using the Code view of the Document window**			
9.1.1	Using the Wrap Tag option to edit HTML source code	Basic	Unit 6, Topic D	D-1
9.1.2	Collapsing and expanding selected sections of code	Basic	Unit 6, Topic D	D-1
9.1.3	Applying and removing comments	Basic	Unit 6, Topic D	D-1
9.1.4	Using code hints by typing <, /, or pressing the spacebar	Basic	Unit 6, Topic D	D-1
9.2	**Making changes to code using Design view of the Document window**			
9.2.1	Using Quick Tag Editor to insert or wrap code around a tag	Basic	Unit 6, Topic E	E-1
9.2.2	Right-clicking and choosing Edit Tag to invoke the dialog box	Basic	Unit 6, Topic E	E-1
9.3	**Selecting specific code**			
9.3.1	Working with the Code Navigator	Basic	Unit 6, Topic C	C-1
9.3.2	Using the Tag selector to select tags in a nested hierarchy	Basic	Unit 6, Topic C	C-1
9.3.3	Using Find and Replace to find a specific tag	Basic	Unit 6, Topic F	
9.4	**Understanding related files**			
9.4.1	Types of related files: CSS, SSI, JavaScript, Spry data, XML	Basic	Unit 1, Topic C	
		Advanced	Unit 7, Topic A	A-1
9.4.2	Selecting related files by clicking tabs in Document window	Basic	Unit 1, Topic C	C-3
9.5	**Working with behaviors**			
9.5.1	Understanding behaviors (user interaction provokes actions)	Advanced	Unit 4, Topic A	
9.5.2	Understanding events (onClick, onMouseOver, etc.)	Advanced	Unit 4, Topic A	
9.5.3	Using the Tag Inspector panel to apply behaviors to tags	Advanced	Unit 4, Topic A	A-1
9.5.4	Changing the order of applied behaviors	Advanced	Unit 4, Topic A	A-1
9.5.5	Deleting behaviors previously applied to tags	Advanced	Unit 4, Topic A	

10 Working with templates and library items

#	Objective	Course level	Conceptual information	Supporting activities
10.1	**Creating and applying templates**			
10.1.1	Understanding that templates contain common elements	Advanced	Unit 3, Topic B	
10.1.2	Creating new templates in New Document dialog box	Advanced	Unit 3, Topic B	B-1
10.1.3	Creating pages from templates in New Document dialog box	Advanced	Unit 3, Topic B	B-3
		Advanced	Unit 7, Topic A	A-1
10.2	**Inserting editable regions**			
10.2.1	Inserting editable regions to define areas of page content	Advanced	Unit 3, Topic B	B-1
10.3	**Editing and updating templates**			
10.3.1	Editing templates by opening up the DWT file directly	Advanced	Unit 3, Topic B	B-5
10.3.2	Updating all pages that are based on an edited template	Advanced	Unit 3, Topic B	B-5
10.4	**Creating and editing Library items**			
10.4.1	Understanding that Library items are reusable code chunks	Advanced	Unit 3, Topic A	A-1, A-3
10.4.2	Using the New Document dialog box to create Library items	Advanced	Unit 3, Topic A	
10.4.3	Using the Assets panel to create Library items	Advanced	Unit 3, Topic A	A-1
10.4.4	Editing Library items	Advanced	Unit 3, Topic A	A-2
10.4.5	Inserting Library items	Advanced	Unit 3, Topic A	A-1

11 Working with mobile devices

#	Objective	Course level	Conceptual information	Supporting activities
11.1	**Using jQuery Mobile**			
11.1.1	Creating new jQuery Mobile files (New>Page from samples)	Advanced	Unit 7, Topic A	A-1
11.1.2	Applying swatches with the jQuery Mobile Swatches panel	Advanced	Unit 7, Topic A	A-2

#	Objective	Course level	Conceptual information	Supporting activities
11.2	**Understanding PhoneGap**			
11.2.1	Understanding that PhoneGap builds native apps for mobile	Advanced	Unit 7, Topic B	B-1
11.2.2	Using PhoneGap Build Service panel to emulate mobile app	Advanced	Unit 7, Topic B	
11.2.3	Using PhoneGap Build Service to share app builds	Advanced	Unit 7, Topic B	

12 Launching a site

#	Objective	Course level	Conceptual information	Supporting activities
12.1	**Transferring files by using Get and Put**			
12.1.1	Understanding the difference between Get and Put	Basic	Unit 7, Topic C	C-1
12.1.2	Choosing whether to upload dependent files	Basic	Unit 7, Topic C	
12.2	**Understanding and using Check In/Check Out**			
12.2.1	Enabling Check In/Check Out in Advanced Site Setup dialog	Basic	Unit 7, Topic C	C-2
12.2.2	Using Check In/Check Out to enable team collaboration	Basic	Unit 7, Topic C	C-2
12.2.3	Overriding the Check Out feature to access locked files	Basic	Unit 7, Topic C	
12.3	**Uploading a site using the Files panel**			
12.3.1	Understanding the differences between Remote and Local	Basic	Unit 7, Topic C	C-1
12.3.2	Expanding and collapsing the Files panel to see both panes	Basic	Unit 7, Topic C	C-1
12.3.3	Selecting the site's root folder to Put or Get the entire sits	Basic	Unit 7, Topic C	

Course summary

This summary contains information to help you bring the course to a successful conclusion. Using this information, you will be able to:

A Use the summary text to reinforce what you've learned in class.

B Determine the next course in this series, as well as any other resources that might help you continue to learn about Dreamweaver CS6.

Topic A: Course summary

Use the following summary text to reinforce what you've learned in class.

Unit summaries

Unit 1

In this unit, you learned the basics of the Internet and HTML, and that Dreamweaver uses XHTML code by default. Then, you identified the main components of the **Dreamweaver CS6 workspace**. Next, you learned how to switch **views** in the Document window and performed some basic **text editing**. You also used the **Property inspector** and switched between the HTML and CSS sections. Finally, you learned how to **preview** a page in a browser and how to set the primary and secondary preview browsers.

Unit 2

In this unit, you learned how to **plan a website** before building it. Then, you learned how to define a **local site** and set the **local root folder**. Next, you **created a new web page** as well as set the default document type and page extension. Finally, you also learned how to use the **Files panel** to **organize site files** and folders.

Unit 3

In this unit, you learned how to **add text** from other sources. You also learned about **special characters** and how to insert these characters into the HTML code. Next, you learned how to apply **structural tags**. Then, you learned how to insert a **paragraph break** and **a line break** in code. Finally, you learned how to create and nest **lists**.

Unit 4

In this unit, you explored **CSS** basics. You learned how to create and use an **external style sheet**. Next, you defined and applied **element styles** and **class styles**. Finally, you explored the concepts of the **cacade effect**, **inheritance**, and learned how to use the `!important` statement.

Unit 5

In this unit, you learned how to insert **image files** as well as how to set mage **attributes**, use **placeholders**, and create **rollovers**. Next, you learned how to use **basic editing tools** available on the Properties inspector and how to access an **external image editor** from Dreamweaver. You also learned how to add **Flash** files. Then, you explored **links types**, link **target** options, and types of link **paths** as well as how to **create links**.

Unit 6

In this unit, you learned more about **HTML**, **XHTML**, and **HTML5**. Then, you explored what is contained within the `<head>` section. Next, you used the **Code Navigator** and **tag selector**. You also used the Coding toolbar in Code view. Next, you learned how to use the **Quick Tag Editor** in Design view. Finally, you learned how to use the **Find and Replace** tool to replace content and code.

Unit 7

In this unit, you learned how to prepare a website to be published and checking spelling. Then, you learned the basics of **website publishing** with Dreamweaver. Finally, you learned how to **upload local files** to a remote site, use **Put** or **Get** to upload or download the entire site, and how to use the **Check In/Check Out** feature to avoid file version control problems.

Topic B: Continued learning after class

It is impossible to learn how to use any software effectively in a single day. To get the most out of this class, students should begin working with Dreamweaver CS6 to perform real tasks as soon as possible. We also offer resources for continued learning.

Next courses in this series

This is the first course in this series. The next course in this series is:

- *Dreamweaver CS6: Advanced, ACE Edition*

Other resources

For more information on this and other topics, go to **www.Crisp360.com**.

Crisp360 is an online community where you can expand your knowledge base, connect with other professionals, and purchase individual training solutions.

Glossary

Cascading Style Sheets (CSS)
Used to format HTML content and control the positioning of various page elements.

Class styles
CSS style rules that use class selectors, which allow you to give elements names that are relevant to your document structure. You can apply class styles to multiple elements on a page.

Cloaking
Defining a file(s) or folder(s) as cloaked allows you to store them in your site but prevents them from being included in normal site operations, such as link reports or uploading functions.

Definition list
An HTML list used for structuring terms and their corresponding definitions. Often used for glossaries, pages of frequently asked questions (FAQs), and similar contexts

Dependent files
Assets and other files that are referenced by the HTML file.

Deprecated tags
Tags that are discouraged in favor of newer, better options. For example, the `<font>` tag in older versions of HTML is now deprecated in favor of CSS.

Element styles
CSS style rules that use tag selectors to define the formatting of HTML elements, such as headings and paragraphs. An element style overrides any default formatting for an HTML element.

External links
Links to a page or resource outside a Web site.

External style sheet
A text file that is saved with a .css extension and that contains style rules that define how various HTML elements are displayed.

Font set
A group of similar typefaces that help ensure consistent text display in a variety of browsers and operating systems.

GIF
An image file format that can support a maximum of 256 colors. GIF files are best used for images with relatively few colors and with areas of flat color, such as line drawings, logos, and illustrations.

Hexadecimal color values
A three- or six-digit code that starts with the pound sign (#) and specifies the combination of red, green, and blue to display the color seen on a computer screen.

HTML
Hypertext Markup Language, the standard markup language on the Web. HTML consists of *tags* that define the basic structure of a Web page.

HTML validation
Comparing your web page(s) to the standards defined by the World Wide Web Consortium (W3C).

Internal links
Links to pages or resources within a Web site.

Internet
A vast array of networks that belong to universities, businesses, organizations, governments, and individuals all over the world.

JPEG
An image file format that supports more than 16 million colors. JPEG is best used for photographs and images that have many subtle color shadings.

Link states
The four states, or conditions, that a link can be in: link, hover, active, and visited.

Local site
A folder on your computer where you work on the website before it is published to a web server.

Margin
The space between page content and the edge of the browser window, or the space between individual elements.

Monospaced font
A typeface in which every character uses the same amount of space. For example, an "i" and an "m" take up the same amount of space on a line. Monospaced fonts, such as Courier, resemble typewriter text.

Named anchor
A code reference you can target as a link within a document. Named anchors are also called bookmark links or intra-document links.

Nested list
Also called a sub-list, a list that starts inside a list item tag of another list. Nested lists are used when you need to create indented sub-lists within a larger list.

Nonbreaking space

A special HTML character that inserts a single space without breaking a line.

Ordered list

An HTML list structure that automatically appends sequential labels to each list item. By default, list items are numbered 1, 2, 3, and so on.

Orphaned files

Files that reside in your site folders but aren't linked to by any pages.

PNG

An image file format that combines some of the best features of JPEG and GIF. The PNG format supports more than 16 million colors and supports many levels of transparency. However, many older browsers don't fully support the PNG format.

Remote site

When the website is ready for your intended audience, you copy the site files from the local folder to this folder on a web server.

Sans serif font

A typeface whose characters don't have serifs (flourishes or ornaments at the ends of the strokes that make up the letters).

Serif font

A typeface whose characters have serifs (flourishes or ornaments at the ends of the strokes that make up the letters).

Special characters

Symbols or language-specific characters that require HTML code to be displayed on a web page. The code begins with an ampersand (&) and end with a semicolon. For example, © displays the copyright symbol (©) on a web page.

Synchronization

Comparing local and remotes files by the time stamps saved with each file to identify the latest version.

Unordered list

An HTML list structure that automatically appends bullets to each list item. Use this kind of list when the list items aren't sequential and don't need to be in any particular order.

Visual aids

Page icons, symbols, or borders that are visible only in Dreamweaver. You can turn certain visual aids on and off to make it easier to work with the page.

XHTML

Extensible Hypertext Markup Language, a strict version of HTML that doesn't allow proprietary tags or attributes. Instead, all style information is controlled by CSS. XHTML allows for cleaner, more efficient code. By default, Dreamweaver CS5 builds pages with XHTML code.

Index